Design

Design
The Key Concepts

D. J. HUPPATZ

BLOOMSBURY VISUAL ARTS
LONDON · NEW YORK · OXFORD · NEW DELHI · SYDNEY

BLOOMSBURY VISUAL ARTS
Bloomsbury Publishing Plc
50 Bedford Square, London, WC1B 3DP, UK
1385 Broadway, New York, NY 10018, USA

BLOOMSBURY, BLOOMSBURY VISUAL ARTS and the Diana logo are trademarks of Bloomsbury Publishing Plc

First published in Great Britain 2020

© D. J. Huppatz, 2020

D. J. Huppatz has asserted his right under the Copyright, Designs and Patents Act, 1988, to be identified as Author of this work.

For legal purposes the Acknowledgments on p. x constitute an extension of this copyright page.

All rights reserved. No part of this publication may be reproduced or transmitted in any form or by any means, electronic or mechanical, including photocopying, recording, or any information storage or retrieval system, without prior permission in writing from the publishers.

Bloomsbury Publishing Plc does not have any control over, or responsibility for, any third-party websites referred to or in this book. All internet addresses given in this book were correct at the time of going to press. The author and publisher regret any inconvenience caused if addresses have changed or sites have ceased to exist, but can accept no responsibility for any such changes.

Every effort has been made to trace copyright holders of images and to obtain their permission for the use of copyright material. The publisher apologizes for any errors or omissions in copyright acknowledgment and would be grateful if notified of any corrections that should be incorporated in future reprints or editions of this book.

Disclaimer: The corporate brands/logos contained in this book are reproduced under the fair dealing and/or fair use defenses/exceptions under English, US and international copyright laws. In relation to US law, the author and publishers also exercise their rights to publish these logos under the First Amendment to the US Constitution. The author and publishers also rely on the various defenses/exceptions under English, US and international trademark laws.

A catalogue record for this book is available from the British Library.

A catalog record for this book is available from the Library of Congress.

ISBN:	HB:	978-1-3500-6815-5
	PB:	978-1-3500-6814-8
	ePDF:	978-1-3500-6817-9
	ePub:	978-1-3500-6816-2

Series: The Key Concepts

Typeset by Integra Software Services Pvt. Ltd.

To find out more about our authors and books visit www.bloomsbury.com and sign up for our newsletters.

Contents

List of images viii
Acknowledgments x
Preface xi

Introduction 1
    What is design? 1
    Design's relatives 5
    Design's history 8
    The concepts 13

1   Information 17
    From print culture to cyberspace 18
    Making marks 21
    Case study 1: Emojis 24
    Graphic identities 26
    Visualizing data 28
    Finding our way 31
    Case study 2: Infographics 33
    The return to craft 35

2   Things 37
    From mechanization to automation 38
    Serial things 41
    Case study 3: Chairs 44
    Singular things 47
    Materials 49
    Case study 4: KickStart MoneyMaker pump 52
    Ethics 53
    Conclusion 55

3 Interaction 57
　Designing machines for people 58
　Affordances and scripts 60
　Case study 5: The door 63
　Interface 65
　Software 67
　Case study 6: The iPhone 70
　Smart things 72
　Robots 74

4 Systems and Services 79
　Systems 80
　Case study 7: IKEA 83
　Mapping services 84
　Sharing 88
　Case study 8: Uber 90
　Hackathons and jams 91
　Social design 93
　Government services 95
　Conclusion 96

5 Experiences 99
　Interaction and emotion 99
　Participation and co-creation 102
　Case study 9: Facebook 106
　Inclusive experience 108
　Case study 10: Universal design 110
　The experience economy 112
　Immersive entertainment 114
　Tourism 116
　Conclusion 118

6 Strategies 121
　Organizational design 121
　Case study 11: IBM 125
　Strategic design 126
　Policy 130

Problems and methods 133
Case study 12: IDEO 135
Design thinking 136

Conclusion 141

Design in the Anthropocene 141
Technological fixations 144
Design futures 146

Notes 149
Annotated guide to further reading 161
Select bibliography 167
Index 170

List of images

1. Commuters pass below New York Subway signage in Helvetica. Getty Images: Credit: Christian Science Monitor 3

2. Village guards pose with their AK-47s in the Southeastern Anatolia Region of Turkey, 2015. Getty Images: Credit: Anadolu Agency 4

3. Ofo, a bicycle-sharing app on a smartphone in front of the company's bikes in Shanghai, China, 2017. Getty Images: Photographer: Qilai Shen/Bloomberg 11

4. Emojis on cell phones, Paris, 2015. The "Face with Tears of Joy" is on the far left column, the third row down. Getty Images: Miguel Medina/AFP 25

5. Visual story and infographics of a fire, from the *Boston Globe*, 2012. Getty Images: Graphic by Aaron Atencio and Javier Zarracina/The Boston Globe via Getty Images 34

6. Marc Newson's "Doha Lounge Chair," a 2012 prototype, sold at auction in 2015 for £27,500 ($35,000 US). Getty Images: Credit: Tristan Fewings/Stringer 45

7. A man sits by stacks of white and red monobloc chairs, Yangon, Myanmar, 2016. Getty Images: photo by Tessa Bunney/In Pictures via Getty Images 46

LIST OF IMAGES

8 Signs indicate how to use the doors of a New York office building. Getty Images/Corbis Historical/James Leynse 64

9 The first generation iPhone, 2007. Getty Images/Axel Schmidt 71

10 Self-serve shelves in IKEA, Miami, 2017. Getty Images/Jeffrey Greenberg/UIG 84

11 A woman passing by an Uber advertisement in Kuala Lumpur, Malaysia, 2018. Getty Images/Faris Hadzig/SOPA Images/Lightrocket 90

12 A picture taken in Moscow on March 22, 2018 shows the Russian language version of Facebook about page featuring the face of founder and CEO Mark Zuckerberg. MLADEN ANTONOV/AFP/Getty Images 107

13 A cluster of raised dots, a tactile feature to help the visually impaired, sit on the new UK 10-pound banknote, 2017. Getty Images: Credit: Bloomberg 111

14 Robert "WATSON" from IBM at the annual Mobile World Congress, 2016. Getty Images: Matthias Oesterle/Corbis Images 125

15 Fans compete for prizes at the Common joins Bank of America's Keep the Change Event, Chicago, 2008. Getty Images/Barry Brecheisen/WireImage 136

16 Chinese men walk past the abandoned share bicycles stored at a temporary parking lot in Shanghai on August 24, 2017. CHANDAN KHANNA/AFP/Getty Images 143

Acknowledgments

Although this is a relatively short book, it represents an accumulation of ideas from many sources. While most of these are collected in the bibliography (the remainder can be found in my *Design: Critical and Primary Sources*), I also owe a number of personal debts to people who have helped me with this book over the past two years.

First is to the Bloomsbury team, particularly Rebecca Barden for commissioning this book and for her ongoing support. Claire Constable provided useful feedback on an early draft and has been equally supportive and encouraging. Thanks also to the anonymous reviewer for their thoughtful appraisal.

Katherine Hepworth offered generous feedback, particularly on Chapter 1, and Stefanie di Russo's thesis was an invaluable source for Chapter 6.

I have also learned a great deal from colleagues and students at Swinburne University of Technology's Architecture and Design School, not only over the past two years, but also over the past decade. Thank you all.

Harry Huppatz and Zeke Huppatz deserve special thanks for their image selections, and this project would not have been possible without Siobhan's ongoing support.

Finally, special thanks to my mother who taught me how to read and write. And dad helped too.

Preface

Design: The Key Concepts introduces design's major themes to newcomers and students interested in graphic, industrial, interactive, interior, service, and systems design, as well as architecture and engineering. Design practitioners, students, and academics have few resources to bridge these various disciplines and fields. Through examining recurring themes, *Design: The Key Concepts* highlights the interconnections between these various manifestations of contemporary design in an accessible and engaging way.

This is not a "how to" book of design techniques. Instead, *Design: The Key Concepts* provides a framework for understanding fundamental issues such as interaction, emotion, sustainability, accessibility, and participation. A series of short case studies illustrate how aspects of design affect our everyday lives. Focusing on concepts and practices developed over the past two decades, *Design: The Key Concepts* aims to be a provocative introduction that challenges conventional ways of thinking about design.

Introduction

Design is everywhere. Every day, we negotiate a world of things, systems, and services that someone has consciously designed. Designers created the apps on our phones, mapped the signage system that helps us navigate the freeway, modeled prototypes for our office furniture, and sketched blueprints for our service systems. To design is to envisage, plan, and—ideally—improve the physical or virtual infrastructure of our lives.

Although design is everywhere, it's often taken for granted. We might notice its final products, when, for example, we come across a website featuring the latest app or innovative new desk lamp. We also notice design when the app glitches, we cannot assemble our lamp or we miss the freeway exit ramp because the sign was unreadable. As typographer John D. Berry succinctly put it, "Only when the design fails does it draw attention to itself; when it succeeds, it's invisible."[1] My aim in this book is to make design visible by mapping its many activities and dimensions in a concise and accessible way.

What is design?

A deceptively simple word, design has various origins. In English, one possible origin is the Latin word *designare*, meaning to mark out, define, or designate. Another, the Italian word *disegno* was used by Renaissance artists to refer to a drawing, pattern, or plan. These origins left us with a twofold meaning for design: an action *and* an outcome. Importantly, both carry an association with an *ideal*. That is, design is the planning, creation, or invention of something that is not just new, but *better* than what currently exists.

Dictionaries typically offer two definitions for design: a verb that refers to the activity of imagining, drafting, sketching, or making plans for a product, building, garment, or system; and a noun that refers to *either* the resulting drafts, sketches, instructions, or plans *or* the finished product. And, if that is not confusing enough, the word *designer* refers to both a person who designs something, and, as an adjective, it denotes something fashionable, prestigious, or luxurious (as in "designer jeans"). Unfortunately, the latter definition caught hold in the popular imagination, particularly in the late twentieth century, leading many people to still associate design with something tasteful, expensive, and exclusive. But this perception is changing.

Design is a fluid term, and its meaning depends on who uses it and in what context it is used. Not only do various design professionals—communication, industrial, interior and interaction designers, as well as architects and engineers—use the word design differently, but also artists, scientists, and politicians use it in yet other ways. In this book, I will take a broad and general approach, as I believe design is little understood outside professional circles, yet vitally important across a range of fields.

So, to attempt an initial definition: to design is to conceive a purpose, plan, and generate possibilities for an action aimed at a particular outcome. Design thus combines both reflection on the present situation and projection into the future. But, to avoid the idea that design could be any kind of action or outcome, we could add the concept that designers plan actions and generate outcomes that aim to *improve* the human experience.

Consider an example. In 1956, Eduard Hoffmann, of the Haas type foundry in Switzerland, commissioned Max Miedinger to design a new typeface that would be consistent, functional, and legible.[2] Miedinger stripped away the superfluous ornament (the serifs) to create a more efficient, rational typeface composed of simple, geometric letters. He called it Helvetica. In the 1960s, through printers' offices, publications, advertisements, and posters, Helvetica spread to become perhaps the world's most popular typeface. Major global companies such as Lufthansa, American Airlines, Toyota, and Panasonic used Helvetica (and its many variants) in their logos and communications. Helvetica featured in signage for government offices, hospitals, airports, and the New York Subway (Figure 1). Sixty years later, the global reach and longevity of this simple typeface suggest that Hoffmann and Miedinger successfully improved our lives by enabling clear and consistent communication.

But, there is a tendency (particularly among design professionals and educators) to emphasize design's role in improving peoples' lives. While this is admirable, in order for our definition of design to hold, we may need to ignore many things that were designed—and, in some cases, very thoughtfully and carefully designed. Despite the best intentions of designers and their clients, the outcomes or end products of design activities do not always improve the human experience. Or, they may only improve life for some people while

FIGURE 1 *Commuters pass below New York Subway signage in Helvetica. Getty Images: Credit: Christian Science Monitor.*

making it worse for others. It is therefore important to acknowledge that design does not always make the world a better place.

Consider another example. In 1945, a young, self-taught designer began work on a prototype for a new assault rifle that improved upon existing weapons used by the Russian army.[3] Mikhail Kalashnikov's design—named the AK-47—was easy to use and cheap to manufacture (Figure 2). First mass produced for the Russian army in 1949, the AK-47 proved reliable and robust on battlefields, so Soviet-allied armies from China to Yugoslavia soon copied and manufactured it. By the end of the twentieth century, it was perhaps the world's most popular assault rifle (it's estimated that 80 to 100 million of them were produced). In terms of its purpose and number of units produced, the AK-47 was certainly successful. But, while Kalashnikov always said that he designed the AK-47 to enable the Red Army to better defend Russia, just before his death in 2013 he expressed regret that his design had been so successful in killing so many people around the world.

Although these two examples identify specific designers, a designed product is rarely the creation—or the sole responsibility—of a single person. In both cases, the designers drew upon existing models and developed their ideas in collaboration with others. Their initial designs (sketches, plans, intentions) also changed during the process to become the final outcome (a typeface, a weapon). In the mid-twentieth century, both designers and their

FIGURE 2 *Village guards pose with their AK-47s in the Southeastern Anatolia Region of Turkey, 2015. Getty Images: Credit: Anadolu Agency.*

users considered Helvetica and the AK-47 as significant improvements on existing options. Over decades, subsequent designers modified, customized, and upgraded the original designs so that Helvetica and the AK-47 are still used today.

For most people, such design activities are invisible and, in complex projects, difficult to visualize. The smartphone, for example, appears to us as a seamless and effortless device, yet an enormous repository of knowledge and range of skills went into conceiving, prototyping, and producing it. Its design process involved collaboration between industrial designers (to create a usable and attractive handset), graphic and interactive designers (to arrange and order visual displays of icons, menus, and information), and software designers (to create the many programs running behind the screen). User testing and research informed design decisions at each level. The apparent simplicity of so many contemporary digital products belies the fact that they are the consequence of many decisions by many designers.

For much of the twentieth century, "form follows function," a phrase originally coined by architect Louis Sullivan, was a standard starting point for modern design practice.[4] Ideally, a product's function (or use) should determine its final form or outcome. But this dictum falters when we consider twenty-first-century products such as a smartphone. What is its function? The first commercial cell phones of the 1980s had a single function—communication—yet after the launch of Apple's popular iPhone in 2007, smartphones included entertainment, navigation, and education as other functions. A smartphone not only embodies various fields of design—product, graphic, interface, and information design—but also operates within broader designed systems and services. In a sense, the smartphone's design is deceptive, as it makes an extremely sophisticated device with multiple functions appear seductively simple.

Design's relatives

The stereotypical image of the designer as a creative loner, obsessively sketching new chairs or logos on a cafe napkin, is an unrealistic one. Design is a profession characterized by its collaborative and consultative nature, and design processes include mediating, judging, and choosing between possible solutions within the limitations and expectations of a project brief. This process typically involves research into materials, production processes and user needs, exploring multiple possibilities, experimenting with prototypes, refining, and testing. This can be a long and frustrating process, each iteration inching closer to a better—or at least a workable—solution.

So, are designers actually artists, engineers, or inventors? So far, we have established the idea that designers plan, prototype, and produce useful things that (hopefully) improve the quality of our lives. But is a designer an imaginative dreamer who works from intuition and imagination like an artist, or more of a technician who works systematically and logically like a scientist? Or is a designer more like a manager, a facilitator who creates structures, relationships, or processes for others? We will explore these questions below by considering design's relationship with its related disciplines.

Art and craft

Many people assume art and design are siblings. Websites, blogs, and books featuring "designer" products, furniture, interiors, or fashion seem to confirm the idea that designers simply "make things look good." But aesthetics represents only a small fraction of design practice. While artists and designers typically share an understanding of basic aesthetic principles, such as balance, form, scale, color, space, and proportion, they each use them differently. Unlike artists, designers rarely value individual expression and design's final outcome is not a unique, rarefied object for contemplation but a useful one that allows someone to do something. If art is concerned with *expressing* the human experience, design is concerned with *enabling* it.

As with art, design shares some common characteristics with craft, particularly an attention to the technical aspect of making things. Usually associated with a single artisan's small-scale production, craft is founded on manual skill as opposed to repetitive mass production.[5] In contrast, designers engage with various technologies, processes, and production scales, and do not necessarily execute the final product. Where crafts practitioners begin with an intimate knowledge of materials or forms, designers begin with clients or users and their needs or desires. This means that designers rarely define the aims of a design project—both aims and outcomes are typically constrained by others. Unlike art and craft, design necessarily requires discussion, negotiation, and compromise.

Museums—and occasionally art galleries and art fairs—display designed objects such as furniture, household items, posters, or products as if they were a type of "useful" art. By their nature, museums collect and exhibit aesthetically pleasing or significant objects, preferably rare and valuable ones. In a museum or gallery context, designed objects are typically arranged by reference to significant styles (such as Art Deco, Modernism, or Postmodernism) or celebrated individuals (such as Frank Lloyd Wright, Marcel Breuer, or Zaha Hadid). The iterative processes, collaborative activities, and production methods involved in designing and manufacturing a piece of furniture, a poster, or a building are lost. Visitors encounter designed objects as exceptional, singular things, exiled from their useful, everyday existence. Unfortunately, this serves to reinforce an unrealistic image of design as a kind of applied art.

Engineering and architecture

Along with art and craft, many people associate design with engineering and architecture. Beyond their technical differences, engineering and architecture share an approach that includes creative thinking, planning, and filtering possibilities to generate the best possible computer system or apartment building. Engineering and architecture draw on specialized technical knowledge, such as mathematics, and the sciences of physical forces and material properties. Both utilize design to mediate between such abstract, scientific knowledge and human use. That is, architects and engineers imagine how people will use a bridge, an office building, or a new software program. Design is an integral part of both disciplines.

If engineering is "creating and using tools to accomplish a task or fulfil a purpose," then this sounds very close to our definition of design.[6] But engineering is often described as an "applied science" and in practice aligns itself close to scientific methods and perspectives. Growing rapidly from its origins in the mid-nineteenth century, engineering now comprises dozens of sub-disciplines. These include civil engineering (designing physical infrastructure), mechanical and electrical engineering (designing machines including automobiles and airplanes), and software and hardware engineering (designing computing components). Today, engineers tend to work within or for specific industries—mining, construction, medical, or chemical industries, for example—and their practice is extremely technical and specialized, often resulting in a lack of consideration for design.

Like engineers, architects consider their discipline as one dedicated to improving the human condition, specifically through constructing our built environment.[7] This includes housing, offices, schools, hospitals, and shops. Professionally, architecture developed a specialized language and education devoted to design and construction. Unfortunately, many architects and critics associate the term "architectural design" specifically with architecture's aesthetic dimension. But, more than this, design is what connects the technical and technological with the human. That is, design is fundamentally concerned with how people use a building, how they interact with its technological and environmental systems, and how they interact with each other within it.

On a practical level, engineering and architecture are unique among the design disciplines as they have a professional status. In most countries, practitioners must gain both a higher degree and accreditation by a professional organization. Engineering and architecture also have long-established institutions and standards, whereas other design professions are relative newcomers. This lack of professional accreditation for other designers can be seen as both a curse and a blessing. Without formal accreditation, graphic, industrial, interior, and interaction designers, for example, lack professional credibility. At the same time, without professional constraints and standardized methods, these designers currently have greater opportunities for interdisciplinary movement and collaboration.

Branding and advertising

Another common connection many people make is between design, branding, and advertising. Usually associated with marketing and promotional activities, design, in this context, is understood as a means to increase exposure or profits for a corporation or an organization. Advertising creatives draw on much of the same visual language and skills as communication or interaction designers, and there is a significant cross-over between them. But, with its purpose of promoting goods or services, advertising's aim is ultimately to influence consumers rather than to improve their quality of life. Having said that, a well-designed advertisement for a health service, for instance, may do both.

Organizations have long understood the importance of branding as a means of identification and promotion. A distinctive visual identity in the form of a logo, packaging, and a website differentiates one company from its competitor. A coherent visual identity can also express the values of a particular product, service, or company. The need for consistency and careful planning of such branding activities have long-provided work for designers. Contemporary corporations, government institutions, educational, sporting, and other organizations consider a holistic approach to designing and maintaining a coherent visual identity essential. There is considerable overlap between the practices of branding, advertising and communication, interaction and information design.

Management

If management is the organization and coordination of people, resources, and activities in order to achieve defined objectives, then this sounds similar to our initial definition of design.[8] And again, there is some overlap between the role of a designer and that of a project manager, for example. But, in the corporate realm, the typical management emphasis on profit, analytics, and quantitative methods of evaluation often neglects the human experience of their products or services. Design offers a human-centered perspective that has gained some attention recently within management circles. Over the past decade, major corporations, governments, and other organizations have deployed design thinking as a potential means to reconfigure their way of doing business and refocus on human needs and desires.

On another level, fields such as organizational or strategic design, with an emphasis on analyzing scenarios or modeling futures, are also affecting management culture. Some designers have extended this into government policy design, with the idea of co-creating processes with a broad public comprising not simply voting citizens, but also individuals with particular needs and desires. In large organizations and governments, such design activities can be difficult to visualize—rather than a chair, an app, or a sign, the final product may be a new policy document or series of policies directed toward a particular outcome. As with the smartphone, the more complex and interconnected our institutions become, the more important it is to carefully design them.

Design's history

Although this is not a book on the history of design—there are numerous such books—it is useful to understand some key ideas from two defining periods that preceded contemporary design practice and thinking. Borrowing from related disciplines, I will refer to these as the period of Industrial Modernization, spanning from the beginning of the Industrial Revolution to the end of Second World War (c.1750–1945) and Accelerated Modernization, corresponding to the five decades from 1945 until the twenty-first century (1945–2000). This is a quick and useful means to map design's trajectory over the past 250 years, from the beginning of what scientists now refer to as the Anthropocene (a topic to which we will return in the Conclusion).

Industrial Modernization is a term that captures the relentless technological, social, and cultural changes that shaped and reshaped the world from the mid-eighteenth to the mid-twentieth centuries. Fueled by steam-powered machines, imperial expansion (British, French, and other European empires), urbanization, mass communication (newspapers and the telegraph), and new forms of transportation (steam-ships and railways), Industrial Modernization had a profound impact on human life. The dialogue between new industrial technologies and human use became a cornerstone of modern design practice. How to control and order the complexity of modern life became one of its key themes.

Beginning in England in the 1830s, government-led Schools of Design, the *Journal of Design and Manufactures*, and the first patent laws for designed products structured the framework for industrial design as a profession. At the same time, engineers designed railway systems and steamships, while architects designed new railway stations and department stores from industrially produced materials, such as cast iron and glass. Urban planners redesigned cities for the emerging, industrially driven world. In the United States, the "American System" of mass manufacturing using standard, interchangeable parts, led initially by the military and agricultural industries, soon churned out masses of affordable consumer items, from clocks and sewing machines to bicycles.

Modern design practice and education in the early twentieth century—exemplified by the Bauhaus in the 1920s and 1930s—were both a response to Industrial Modernization and a driver of it. Industrial designers styled mass-produced consumer items such as furniture, telephones, and radios, while graphic artists designed posters, newspapers, and magazines. From trains and ships to airplanes and automobiles, modern machines needed designing and redesigning with changes in technological possibilities, materials, and people's needs. Architects and engineers continued to create the physical infrastructure of modern cities—from apartment complexes to highway systems—to enable efficient, affordable, and comfortable lives for mass populations.

After the Second World War, the forces unleashed by the Industrial Revolution shifted to another register in the period of Accelerated Modernization. Innovation in materials—reinforced concrete, metallic alloys, plastics, and synthetic fibers—created numerous new possibilities for designers. The speed and volume of communication and transportation continued to accelerate with the spread of television, automobiles, and jet travel. Meanwhile, the accelerated consumption of natural materials and the global spread of industrial manufacturing resulted in both rapid economic growth and the massive consumption of resources. This acceleration—along with industrialized agriculture and advances in health—contributed to a rapid expansion in the world's population from 2.5 billion in 1950 to over 6 billion in 2000.[9] The scale and complexity of design problems were expanding.

In the decades following the Second World War, the professionalization of design developed across a broad front. Specialist education, professional societies, and publications increased as opportunities for design expanded within an increasingly complex and interconnected world. An earlier emphasis on styling mass-produced objects and publications gave way to planning or conceptualizing systems, services, or scenarios as design shifted from tangible to intangible things. Efforts to establish professional respectability for designers resulted in a wave of design theories and scientific approaches to the discipline. Design's independence from art and science, its alliance to consumerism, marketing, and promotion, its relationship to management, and its role in systems and services emerged as significant themes during the last decades of the twentieth century.

The first two decades of the twenty-first century brought further significant change, mainly due to digital technologies. As at 2017, for example, 77 percent of Americans owned smartphones, and for some countries (such as South Korea), the percentage was higher.[10] And, although there is still a significant digital divide between wealthy and poorer countries, 40 percent of world's population can now access the internet, and the majority do so through smartphones.[11] Considering that a little more than a decade ago, nobody owned a smartphone, this is a revolutionary change. Since the 1990s, increased connectivity to digital networks has changed design and daily life in profound ways—not only due to new digital devices but also due to the redesign of services and systems in response to such devices.

For designers, the past two decades have seen design activities spread in various directions, including into new realms such as interactive, service, and experience design. Artificial intelligence (AI), digital prosthetics, genetic engineering, and the Internet of Things promise to change human experiences ever more rapidly over the next two decades. Regardless of how such technologies unfold, design's role remains essential in not only shaping such technologies but also adapting our lives to the new situations they create.

Currently, this includes a shift from designing more material things (and therefore using more resources and energy) to designing services and experiences that take advantage of existing products, systems, or infrastructure. Rather than design a new bicycle for mass manufacture, for example, designers might develop a better bicycle-sharing service accessible via a smartphone (Figure 3). Rather than each individual owning a product and using it only occasionally, such services are premised on the idea of sharing resources and using them only when we need them. At the intersection of service design and interaction design, product design and existing infrastructure, such a design project is an example of the increasing importance of interdisciplinary practice.

It is easy to point to the tangible outcomes of design—Helvetica or the AK-47—yet, in the past twenty years, the virtual realm that shapes our lives in invisible ways has become an increasingly important focus for designers. Large consultancies such as IDEO and Frog Design have expanded their practices from designing products, packaging, and websites to interaction, service, and experience design. Although these new design fields may

FIGURE 3 *Ofo, a bicycle-sharing app on a smartphone in front of the company's bikes in Shanghai, China, 2017. Getty Images: Photographer: Qilai Shen/ Bloomberg.*

include physical outcomes, creating new things in the physical realm is not necessarily the ultimate aim of much contemporary design practice. Even a discrete physical product is inseparable from the digital realm. Designing a new bicycle, for example, requires an accompanying website, branding, and advertising in order to reach a large audience.

Design in an age of digital commerce, e-books, music and video streaming, and social media presents very different challenges to those faced by twentieth-century designers. Instant communication and information, 3D printing and robotic manufacturing are creating both new possibilities and new challenges for designers. The digital realm promises designers the fantasy and frustrations of total control in which ideal forms appear closer than ever, without the messy materiality of the physical realm. Yet the physical persists, hidden in distant server farms and undersea cables, its infrastructure more complex and interrelated, even as digital computing enters into every conceivable aspect of contemporary life.

That said, trajectories that began with the Industrial Revolution have continued into the twenty-first century. Population growth, urbanization, climate change, deforestation, and species extinction are accelerating with greater intensity and pose ever-greater challenges. For the twenty-first-century designer, while "form follows function" and visualization skills are no longer sufficient, basic questions remain a good starting point. What do people really need? As well as keeping up-to-date with technological change, today's designers need to interview, consult, collect data, and understand users—or work closely with researchers who do. Beyond technical and visual skills, designers need empathy, team-building, problem solving, and narrative skills.

While design cannot solve all of the world's problems, it can make a positive contribution to improving the human condition. In the future, this might be achieved by professional designers or by non-professionals developing their design capabilities. As its effect on our lives is extensive, a basic understanding of design's current state via its key concepts seems a fundamental first step. The chapters that follow are intended to introduce design in its various forms to the widest possible audience.

By examining design in terms of the six concepts outlined below, readers can get a broad overview of its current and future possibilities. These concepts are arranged via "orders" of design, from the design of basic information and simple, discrete things to more complex, intangible systems, services, and experiences.[12] Although conceived on a sliding scale from less to more complex, the order below is not intended to be hierarchical, but overlapping and interacting. And, as we will see, designing a seemingly simple thing can be an incredibly complex process involving multiple teams in a global network.

The concepts

Information

Today, we have access to an ever-increasing volume of data, facts, opinions, and ideas. Designers who can meaningfully shape and structure this mass into useful and usable information provide a vital service. Operating under various names, graphic, communication or information designers use signs, symbols, images, and language to direct, inform, educate, and engage us. Converting raw data into information across digital and print media takes a variety of forms, including logos and visual identities, illustrations and packaging, signage systems, and data visualizations. Designing text and images for these purposes is an essential, if often unnoticed, service that aids us in our everyday lives. Ultimately, designers engaged with information aim to facilitate clear communication that responds to the needs, abilities, and tastes of their audience.

Things

Traditionally, industrial and product designers designed and created mass-produced things, and this remains an essential part of professional practice. In addition to designing useful things, they also aim to create products that are simple to use, safe, sustainable, and pleasurable. But, in the new millennium, the boundaries between mass-produced and singular things, machine-made and hand-crafted things are no longer clear. Enabled by new materials, technologies, and processes, designers in the last two decades have adopted new approaches to designing things. At the intersection of design, engineering, marketing, and manufacturing, designing things is now a complex and collaborative process. The possibilities enabled by 3D printing, robotic manufacturing, and "smart" things connected to digital networks offer a diverse range of options for designers.

Interactions

Even the simplest everyday object—a chair, a book, or a shirt—is designed with an end user in mind. How we interact with such things has long been of interest to designers. Prior experience and patterns of behavior shape our interactions, but at the same time, how things are designed affects our future behaviors and interactions. Since the "digital revolution," the interaction between high-tech products, systems, and their users has become increasingly complex. New fields devoted to interaction with digital products, interface design, and software design have challenged earlier ideas about interaction. Analyzing how we interact with designed products via various levels of user participation reveals design's mediating role between new technologies and their users.

Systems and services

In response to the increasing levels of material "stuff" surrounding us, some designers have shifted their attention away from designing physical products to designing product service systems or services that have very little tangible outcomes. And, given the existence of so many systems we rely on for everyday activities—from digital communication to transportation systems— new products or innovative ways of doing things typically incorporate some kind of existing system or service provision. An overview of systems and service design, including both high-tech and low-tech systems comprising products, services, and their users, reveals the extent of this aspect of contemporary design practice.

Experiences

The often-quoted dictum of good design, "form follows function" is only a starting point when we consider our experience of designed information, products, and systems. Beyond simply use, desire, memory, and emotions are also important considerations that affect a user's interactions with designed things. Our consumption, use, and discard of everyday products are intimately connected to our feelings about them, suggesting profound social, psychological, and even spiritual connections people attach to some things. These connections extend into the virtual realm as our interaction with material objects is increasingly enmeshed with our virtual lives, leading to a more complex understanding of designing for experiences.

Strategies

The integration of products, services, and systems is essential to many of the world's largest companies. How these companies embed design within their organizations to integrate their various functions is the focus of this chapter. Rather than discrete solutions, a strategic design approach works within large-scale systems to identify solutions in areas such as healthcare, education, and climate change. Increasingly, governments and non-profit organizations are also looking to design methods to transform their services and systems in various ways. Through prototyping future scenarios, strategic design is also being applied to diverse areas such as government policy, corporate innovation policies, and the design of "smart cities." In a broader business context, design thinking as a means to expand creativity in organizations and alter the behavior of users is the latest and most popular manifestation of such ideas.

Conclusion: Design in the Anthropocene

In a world characterized by constant change, a broad understanding of design and its processes is a crucial means by which we can shape our future. The stimulation and exchange brought about by global flows of goods, people, and ideas over the past fifty years or so have profoundly affected design practice. While globalization is often characterized as a homogenizing force, it has also encouraged an intensification of the local through an understanding that each culture shapes its own social structures, value systems, and perceptions of reality. Global processes that seem out of control and overwhelming—climate change, for example—are the result of designed processes. By understanding how such processes work, we might redesign or even "undesign" unsustainable products, systems, and practices and redirect efforts toward a desirable future.

Chapter summary

- Design is an almost invisible yet essential part of everyday life
- Although design is complex, its end products appear simple and effortless
- As a practice, design crosses disciplinary boundaries
- Design mediates between new technologies, materials, and people
- Designers can make a vital contribution to a better future

1

Information

In his 1970 best-seller *Future Shock*, Alvin Toffler popularized the phrase "information overload" to describe people's anxiety and disorientation at rapid technological and social change.[1] Fifty years later, the deluge of emails, social media updates, and news posts, not to mention billboards, posters, signs, and paperwork we face daily, makes Toffler's phrase seem either premature or prophetic. Apps that record and quantify our physical activities, nutrition, and mental health through wearable sensors, their data filtered and arranged on a screen as colorful graphs and dynamic charts, distract our attention from the continual stream of news feeds, celebrity gossip, and ads on smartphones. Ours is a society increasingly driven by overwhelming masses of information.

But what is information? And how do we communicate, absorb, and use it? Colloquially, we understand information as the stuff that flows in bits and bytes through our electronic media and appears magically as words and images on our screens. Most people associate information with facts. More precisely, information is knowledge that is communicated or acquired. To inform is to impart concepts, ideas, or facts on a particular subject. The "in" describes the substance, while the "form" describes the structure.[2] Structuring knowledge into a useful format—from a medieval manuscript to a modern poster—has always been central to design.

Management guru Peter Drucker defined information as "data endowed with relevance and purpose."[3] That is, information is *designed data*. Raw data, code, or text is rarely comprehensible, provocative, or engaging. Designers filter, organize, structure, and clarify it to make it readable, attractive, provocative, or inspirational. Ideally, they shape a potential chaos of numbers, words, and images into websites, apps, books, signs, logos, and advertising. In short, information is data packaged into an appropriate format that we can use. And, given our limited processing abilities and shrinking attention spans, design's crucial—yet often unnoticed—role is as important as ever to help overcome our information overload.

A common assumption among the general public is that graphic or communication designers make words and images attractive, as if design is all form and no substance. Their role is often seen as that of visual stylists, whose job is to shape and illustrate information to make it visually appealing. Designer Beatrice Warde, in a 1930 lecture, "Printing Should Be Invisible," proposed a memorable analogy of this idea. Printing and typography, she argued, should be "the unnoticed vehicle for the transmission of ideas," like a crystal goblet that highlights the wine within.[4] But Warde's image only captures part of the story: design is almost invisible yet it is always inseparable from the content. Design, whether a crystal goblet or plastic cup, is worth noticing.

Graphic, communication, or information designers organize visual, textual, and numerical knowledge to make it understandable, usable, and stimulating. Ideally, they shape information in an intelligible and appropriate format. The visual organization of a message "serves to establish clear relations of importance, inclusion, connection, and dependence, and serves as a guide to the sequence in the perception of a message, helping the viewer in the process of constructing meaning."[5] In a world saturated by visual stimuli, creating a clear and engaging visual message is an ongoing challenge faced by designers, particularly given the wide range of media available today.

But it is worth emphasizing that greater transparency, clarity, and simplicity do not necessarily mean faster communication or more efficient transfer of knowledge. The rapid pace of contemporary life and the expectation of instant communication suggest that designers should design information for optimal efficiency and immediate consumption. One recent study revealed that the subtle aspects of designing a page, such as carefully considering its layout, typography, balance, symmetry, spacing, and hierarchy, increased readers' comprehension, focus, and engagement but not the speed at which they read.[6] That is, design does not just order knowledge to enable the most efficient consumption of data. It also inspires, provokes, and delights.

From print culture to cyberspace

Around 1455, Johannes Gutenberg's workshop in Mainz printed a bible using movable metal type. By adopting a uniform shape and size for each letter, and setting the text on a gridded page format, Gutenberg mechanized book design. With further standardization in printing machines, ink, and paper, these new processes soon replaced the painstaking practice of copying manuscripts by hand. By 1500, printers in over a dozen European cities had produced 40,000 editions of books. The "Gutenberg Galaxy" expanded over the next four centuries to incorporate not only religious, but also political and scientific knowledge, as well as news and entertainment.[7] Precise, rapid repetition of text meant information was no longer packaged in singular, expensive manuscripts but disseminated in mass-produced books.

But reading remained an elite pursuit until a truly mass market for printed matter emerged in the nineteenth century. Beginning in England, a wave of mechanization, including steam-powered printing and paper mills, resulted in lower costs and higher volumes. Literacy levels rose and the variety of printed material, including magazines, newspapers, posters, advertising, and packaging, increased. Global communications and transport, including the spread of railways and steam ships, meant faster and wider distribution. This new era of mass publishing required increasingly specialized skills in engraving, illustration, typography, and composition. From within the printing and publishing industries, a new professional known as an applied or commercial artist emerged.

In the twentieth century, printed material became even cheaper to produce and disseminate. From postage stamps to propaganda posters, bank notes to cereal boxes, the variety of printed media that needed to be designed expanded and design became increasingly specialized. Working in advertising, book design, typography, and illustration in Chicago, William Addison Dwiggins was one of the first professionals to describe himself as a "graphic designer." A founder of the American Institute of Graphic Arts (AIGA), Dwiggins wrote regularly on the profession and established early principles for design. "An orderly and graceful disposition of parts," he wrote in 1922, "continues to be desirable and printed pages are still intended to be read."[8] Dwiggins's principles of order and grace to enable communication isolated the design aspect of an otherwise mechanized printing process.

In the 1920s and 1930s, modernist designers such as Jan Tschichold, Herbert Bayer, and Lazlo Moholy-Nagy sought to codify design's visual conventions alongside avant-garde art. Tschichold's influential book, *The New Typography*, for example, promoted principles for graphic designers, such as truth, fitness for purpose, and economy of means, as well as the importance of "standardization, rationalization, and mechanization."[9] Such principles, combined with new design education programs, such as that of Germany's radical Bauhaus, established professional legitimacy for graphic designers. For modernists, graphic design was a studio-based creative practice, still aligned with drawing and painting, yet also in the service of a mass public.

After the Second World War, graphic design continued to grow, with new professional associations, educational institutions, and publications. Widespread color photography, rapid printing processes, and an increase in advertising and branding meant the landscape of urban life was teaming with graphic images and text. Modern corporate logos, advertising, and typography spread globally (as we saw in the Introduction with Helvetica). Designer and educator Paul Rand, who created the iconic logos for IBM and ABC in the 1960s, argued that "good design" shapes the human environment "to reach and to influence the taste of vast audiences."[10] Rand ultimately saw the designer as a form-maker who possessed impeccable taste.

In the twentieth century, graphic designers wavered between an identity as service providers and creative artists. Were they simply fulfilling a client's brief or creating a new cultural form? Ethically, they wondered if graphic design simply encouraged mass consumerism or provided an audience with useful information. Was it ultimately promotion or propaganda? In a 1964 manifesto, "First Things First," British designer Ken Garland, for example, criticized designers who "have flogged their skill and imagination to sell such things as: cat food, stomach powders, detergents, hair restorer, striped toothpaste, aftershave lotion, beforeshave lotion, slimming diet, fattening diets, deodorants, fizzy water, cigarettes, roll-ons, pull-ons and slip-ons."[11] But even as design's social and cultural role was the subject of such debates, new technologies offered alternative processes and visual languages.

In the 1980s and 1990s, personal computing, digital printing, and the internet radically changed design practices and processes. The Apple Macintosh, launched in 1984, enabled graphic designers to work digitally. By the end of the 1990s, sophisticated layout and image-editing software, such as Adobe's Illustrator and Photoshop, combined with desktop publishing programs fundamentally changed design and printing processes. Typesetting, layout, and illustration could now be done at a computer terminal without handling metal type, sketching by hand, or pasting images onto a final proof. Graphic design was no longer the preserve of professionals, as amateurs could now choose fonts, design layouts, and manipulate images to potentially create professional-looking publications.

In the early decades of the twenty-first century, the networked, global, and virtual environment—or cyberspace—also had a profound effect on graphic design. The Gutenberg Galaxy was founded on paper and ink, its knowledge communicated and preserved in books, newspapers, and documents. But in cyberspace, text and images are less fixed than in print, and easier to edit, redesign, and erase. Copying, pasting, and sharing is also easier (and copyright harder to enforce), so that the stability and authority formerly associated with print began to dissolve. For designers, digital type and images presented both new problems and possibilities.

By the 2010s, much of the formerly vast print realm, including newspapers, magazines, and advertising, migrated to online formats or morphed into new forms that incorporated blogs, video content, and social media feeds. From these new forms, designers face new challenges concerning the legitimacy and authenticity of information. Fake news, ads, profiles, and data continue to pose questions as to design's ethical and political role. As graphic design changed to communication design, information design, web design, or user experience design, it became at once more specialized yet also shifted from two to three and four dimensions (the fourth being time). And, while design for print is unlikely to die out, it now comprises only part of professional practice.

Making marks

They are everywhere. From an automobile's dashboard to airport signage, graphic marks instruct us, inform us, and help us in the form of warning symbols, arrows, and bathroom signs. All around the world, people instantly understand the meaning of a sign in a hotel room corridor comprising flames, an arrow, and a person running or a blue sign on a bathroom door with a white stick figure in a wheelchair on it. These images—pictograms—are so ubiquitous that we rarely notice them. Simple, direct and efficient, pictograms may be the simplest form of graphic design. But once you start noticing them, these compact images are a subtle means of communication.

Starting in the mid-1970s, manufacturers and consumers needed symbols for an increasingly global market for technological machines such as stereos, washing machines, and automobiles. Tiny images on buttons and controls could help us operate these machines without the use of text. Pictograms have spread all over our machines and our lives since then. One of the most common is a line within a broken circle: the "Power Symbol." The Power Symbol is part of a collection of standard graphics—a kind of hieroglyphics for the information age—intended for use on technical equipment.[12] The symbol is a combination of 1 and 0, signifying switching between on and off in binary language. Now universally recognized, the symbol has become a global standard, as the words "on" and "off" are not only English-specific, but also take up precious space on our ever-smaller devices.

We know, perhaps without thinking about it, that pressing the "home" button (a stereotypical pitched-roof house) on game consoles, remote controls, and phone apps takes us to the top menu. But for our grandparents, who grew up in a pre-digital era, the tiny images on the remote control look like Egyptian hieroglyphics. That is, such pictograms constitute a contemporary language that is learned through exposure, repetition, or trial and error. And, while we might understand that an image of a wine glass on a cardboard box means "handle with care," the same wine glass printed on a street sign means something quite different. So, pictograms are not only dependent on the users' prior knowledge, but also dependent on where they appear.

Beyond machines, pictograms are used extensively in healthcare, transportation, food retail, and construction. They warn us about occupational hazards such as dangerous machines, fire extinguisher, or exit locations. Ideally, they are not dependent on language to communicate information to people of various cultural backgrounds or education levels. At the same time, the target population must understand their meaning. While the graphic style matters, so do the colors, size, and location—all of this can have an impact on whether they "work" or not.[13] And, in a visually complex world, some pictograms—warning us of danger, for example—must stand out. The appropriate design can even be lifesaving, as in the pictograms on machine operation instructions, vehicle warning lights, or medication warnings.

These seemingly neutral little pictures can also have a significant social and cultural impact. Pictograms are inclusive and exclusive. In America's South during the Jim Crow era, for example, designers created signs to distinguish between drinking fountains, waiting rooms, or store entrances for whites or African Americans. In this way, designed signs consciously conveyed information that enabled racist segregation. Although such signs disappeared in the 1950s and 1960s, yet other politically, culturally, or socially constructed differences remain embedded in our everyday pictographic language. That between genders, for example, is inscribed in the pictograms that depict male and female bathrooms. Where do transgender or non-binary people fit in this sign system?

Along with pictograms, word marks are among the simplest and most familiar visual marks created by designers. In them, text and image are inseparable. Or, more precisely, a word *becomes an image*. Consider Colgate, Visa, Coca-Cola, or Levi's. These words alone are not particularly distinctive or memorable. But when each is rendered in a particular font and color and surrounded by a decorative border, we recognize them instantly. Coca-Cola's distinctive white script on a red background, for instance, is one of the most recognized word marks on the planet. Through repetition in advertising and marketing, we absorb such word marks into our memories as wholes in which text and image are inseparable.

A swoosh on a pair of sneakers, an apple with a bite out of it on the back of a laptop, a bright yellow M rising up in the distance on the highway. Unlike pictograms that instruct, warn, or enable, logos—close relations of word marks—typically encapsulate a particular image or ideal of a company, organization, or institution. Logos are not simply compact visual symbols to advertise corporations but are also essential for government agencies, non-profit organizations, institutions, cities, regions, and nations. And, as with pictograms, these simple visual images can embody social and cultural meanings. The swastika, once an ancient symbol with spiritual significance, became "the graphic embodiment of a heinous dogma that encouraged racist-inspired atrocities" after the German Nazi party adopted it as their official logo.[14] Logos can elicit strong emotions.

The iconic "I heart NY," for example, began in 1976 as a project of the New York State Department of Commerce, Wells Rich Greene advertising agency, and designer Milton Glaser. The campaign was part of a response by the State to New York's financial crisis and the city's reputation for crime and urban blight. The advertising agency already had the tagline "I Love New York," but Glaser created a unique, compact logo from it: a black capital I next to a red heart symbol, followed by a capital N and Y. Used initially in television advertisements, "I heart NY" soon appeared on printed material, T-shirts, and other merchandise. The simple, memorable logo also acquired an emotional investment, particularly with its revival after the 2001 terrorist attack on the city. It also spawned numerous imitations and parodies, and continues to be reproduced over forty years after its creation.

As public marks that are reproduced across our built environment, print media, and online platforms, logos can be loved or hated. When fashion retailer Gap redesigned their logo in 2010, for example, the negative public reaction to the new logo forced the company to quickly return to their old one. In contrast, in 2018, the Cleveland Indians professional baseball team announced it would retire their longstanding logo and mascot "Chief Wahoo" admit controversy over its meaning. Since the 1970s, Native American activists have argued that such logos—part of the visual identity of various sports team and their fans—are racist stereotypes of indigenous people. This ongoing issue of American professional sports teams' use of Native American imagery as part of their visual identity also includes the Washington Redskins, Kansas City Chiefs, and Chicago Blackhawks. Even with their seemingly simple forms, logos are never neutral.

Today, word marks and logos also need to be digital. Susan Kare, a creative director at Apple, designed some of the first widely used digital icons. In 1982, she designed tiny folders for storing documents, a pair of scissors for the "cut" command, and a trash can for clearing clutter. Based on everyday objects that people already knew, these tiny pixelated images enabled users to interact with a computer without knowing any code. Kare's use of everyday objects made computing—an alien world for most people—something relatable, accessible, and fun. After designing the Mac's signature fonts, icons, and graphic interface elements, Kare later designed control panel icons for Microsoft programs and virtual gifts for Facebook. These digital icons are not simply tools but also, combined, form an essential part of how information is organized in our virtual world.

Words are ultimately symbolic marks, and the choice of type—the form of these words—is still an important facet of design practice. Written information, from immigration applications to electricity bills, voting ballots to menus, is ideally designed to be legible and accessible. The visual impression of a page arrests us before we can decipher the words so we know if this is an official document or a light-hearted advertisement immediately. Even at a micro level, the letters themselves create an impression. Times New Roman, for example, a modern homage to the stately lettering inscribed on ancient Roman sculptures, suggested timelessness, seriousness and authority, suitable qualities for a newspaper type. But imagine writing a job application in Comic Sans—not a good choice if you are applying for a job in a law firm. At the same time, Helvetica may not send the right message for your wedding invitation.

Access to language forms is also a matter of inclusion and exclusion. Many indigenous languages do not have specific typefaces, particularly digital ones. In response to this issue, Canadian typographer Raymond Larabie created a new font for the Canadian Government that supports not only the nation's two official languages—English and French—but also over fifty Canadian indigenous alphabets. Originally commissioned to create a geometric typeface for Canada's 150th year celebrations, Larabie also created type for the symbols used in languages such as Cree and Inuktitut. For a form purportedly supposed to represent a unified nation, the Canada 150 font also represents its diversity. The ongoing development of indigenous digital typefaces is part of a broader project of recognition and revitalization, ultimately resulting in means for indigenous people to communicate on their own terms across a variety of digital social media and internet applications.

Finally, the recent development and spread of open-source digital tools may change the possibilities for designers of fonts, icons, and images even further. The design of such visual communication languages, once the realm of professional designers, is becoming more accessible. Font Awesome, for example, offer open-source digital icons for websites, Google Fonts offer open-source web fonts, while GitHub, an online platform for open-source digital projects, includes free access to new graphics, visualization, and image editing tools. While professional graphic and web design software is prohibitively expensive for amateur or causal designers, potentially, such open-source models could provide anyone with the means to design sophisticated digital information.

CASE STUDY 1: EMOJIS

Controversially, the Oxford Dictionaries "Word of the Year" for 2015 was not a word but simple, cartoon-like face expressing happiness. As the year's most popular emoji, the "Face with Tears of Joy" signaled a cultural shift: images were beginning to replace words in everyday digital communication (Figure 4). In social media, Instant Messaging, and SMS people used emojis not just for fun, but

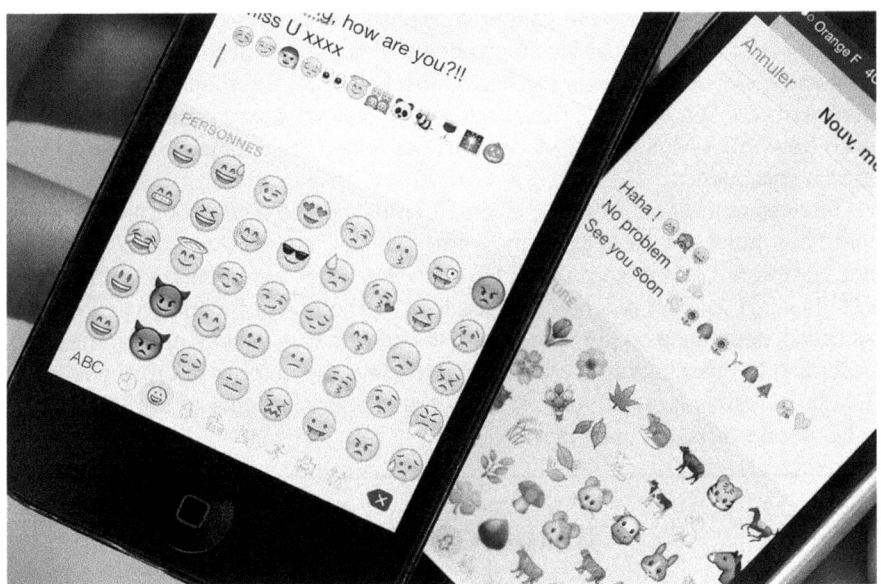

FIGURE 4 *Emojis on cell phones, Paris, 2015. The "Face with Tears of Joy" is on the far left column, the third row down. Getty Images: Miguel Medina/AFP.*

also because they expressed a tone, mood, or emotion that text alone could not. These rapidly evolving digital symbols may become the first global language of cyberspace.

In the 1980s, American techie types created facial expressions using keyboard characters, such as the smiley:-) or wink;-), but emojis developed in Japan as specifically digital images. A Japanese communications firm, NTT DoCoMo, released the original set of 176 emoji (e for "picture" and moji for "character") in 1999 as part of an innovative new service.[15] Influenced by manga characters and pictograms (such as those for the 1964 Tokyo Olympics), designer Shigetaka Kurita created simple icons on a 12 by 12-pixel grid. Over the next decade, emoji use escalated in Japan with increasing mobile communications and more sophisticated digital graphics. In 2011, when Apple integrated its first emoji set for the iPhone, Americans caught the craze.

Text messages lacked the spontaneity of speaking, particularly the tone of voice and accompanying facial expressions. From basic inflections, such as happy or sad, to more complex emotions, such as hope, fear, or sarcasm, emoji added warmth, color, and nuance to what might otherwise be a drab world of electronic text. Their simplicity also meant that emoji quickly crossed cultural and linguistic boundaries and became a global phenomenon. But, in 2010, when the Unicode Consortium produced their first set of standardized emojis for all digital platforms, the white faces, male professionals, and American foods revealed a particular bias.

Why were there no female doctors or dark-skinned policemen? Why sushi and hamburger emojis but none for tacos or empanadas? In response, Emoji 11.0, released in 2018, included female professionals, an extended range of food, and faces that can be altered by skin tone and hair color. Today, over 6 billion emojis are sent on various devices every day and almost half of all comments and captions on Instagram contain emojis.[16] Their widespread cultural acceptance was such that even New York's Museum of Modern Art has added the original emoji set to their design collection.

Yet despite this popularity and diversity, emoji represent emotions and identities that have been pre-packaged—they are, after all, standardized. And emoji are not interpreted in the same way by everyone. How we understand the "Face with Tears of Joy," for example, ranges from humorous or friendly to insincere or sarcastic, depending on the context and the sender. But, despite its fluid meaning, according to Emojitracker, a website that displays the number of emoji posted on Twitter in real-time, as of August 2018, the "Face with Tears of Joy" is still the most popular emoji in use today.

Graphic identities

In January 2008, Barack Obama's campaign to become the Democratic nominee for the US presidential election appeared to be losing ground. His campaign already had a logo, a white rising sun on a blue sky over red-and-white striped fields (that also formed an O for Obama). But his meteoric rise to nominee and then president was encapsulated in a memorable poster designed by Shepard Fairey. Fairey's stylized portrait in a muted red, beige, and blue color scheme depicted Obama in three-quarter view, gazing upward, with the large, bold capital letters HOPE below. It was a classic political pose, yet the simple graphic style suggested street art or stenciling, and the vague one-word statement allowed viewers to project their own meaning (or hope) onto it.

Fairey used a press photograph sourced from Google Images and digital editing tools to design the poster. He cropped, colored, and manipulated the original photograph. And, beyond its immediate use as a poster, placard, or bumper sticker, the image became an internet meme, widely copied, edited, and parodied. Even Fairey himself reused the poster's signature style in his later "We the People" series. Featuring marginalized Americans, such as a Muslim woman wearing a US flag hijab staring directly at the viewer, Fairey's later posters embodied a different type of persuasion, challenging the climate of fear fueled by a new political administration. Memorable, inspirational, and provocative, these images elicit an emotional reaction from their audience.

In a different way, corporate advertising and branding also persuade and aim to embody our hopes, fears, and desires, though usually in more subtle ways. The Japanese retailer Muji, for example, has carefully cultivated a brand that integrates graphic imagery as an essential part of their total aesthetic. Designer Kenya Hara, who took over as art director in 2001, has overseen the design and branding of the minimalist lifestyle corporation, including its logo, advertisements, tag system, product labels for over 7,000 products, and shop signage. Hara's advertisements feature photographs of single bowls, chairs, tables, or products, sharply focused against a neutral grey background or in empty rooms that emphasize their spare, minimal qualities. The ads feature no text apart from the MUJI logo discreetly in a corner.

MUJI's graphic identity, Hara claims, was founded on "emptiness" into which consumers can project their own ideas. "Some think of MUJI as an urban refinement," he explains, "while others think it's about ecology. Some see MUJI as an affordable brand. Others think of it as a reflection of Zen ideology."[17] Without using words, Hara's imagery imbues a mass-produced bowl with all the qualities associated with a traditional Japanese tea room and its ceremony—serenity, simplicity, and raw, understated beauty. MUJI's imagery also appeals directly to global consumers' existing ideas about Japan and their aspirations for a lifestyle that appears modest, ordered, and humble. For busy consumers with complex, technologically driven lives, such imagery projects the simplicity of traditional rituals, an imagined purity and access to a more "authentic" existence through purchasing mass-produced tableware.

In the 2010s, a new wave of online companies attempted to define and redefine their identities via new graphic campaigns and redesigns. Airbnb, for example, changed its brand identity in 2014 with new typography and a new photographic style designed by London-based Design Studio. This consisted of a white, sans-serif font, an abstract logo, and sharp, intimate photographs that suggested snapshots. The consistent, distinctive typeface, colors, icons, and structure made the service seem stable, effortless, and, given its global reach, universal. The designers also emphasized a sense of place, sharing, and connecting with the tagline "belong anywhere." But visual imagery can conceal as much as it reveals, persuading users that an online platform for short-term property rental is really about sharing and belonging. At the same time, we are persuaded that a consistent, universal system can produce unique, local travel experiences.

Branding's origins might lie with ancient Sumerian potters who applied seals to their pottery for trade, to prove their product's authenticity and quality. Or, it may have begun with burning a distinctive symbol onto cows so as to deter theft. These two reasons still apply in the twenty-first century. Today, branding is an essential part of many design projects, and creating a distinctive visual identity is not only crucial for corporations and institutions, but also for cities, nations, and even individuals. Product differentiation and increasingly, legal protection lie at the heart of designing a distinguishing symbol and a distinctive visual language. For designers, creating and maintaining a coherent visual brand might include a logo, printed material, signage, webpage, advertisements, livery, delivery vans, shopping bags, and product packaging.

In the twenty-first century, many people consume products, services, and experiences not only for their functional use, but also for an affiliation with the brand. That is, with their associated social and cultural meanings, brands can help us express our identity, aspirations, or desires. Carrying a distinctive "Tiffany blue" shopping bag around the city signals an aspiration to timeless elegance and luxury, while clutching a McDonald's takeout bag signals an indifference to such aspirations, a less elitist image of cheap, casual consumption. Global brands offer a certain comfort in standardized goods and service—Subway, Coca-Cola, and Google are relatively consistent across the world. Even though their brand meanings are not fixed or static, they do offer some sense of stability in a dynamic world.

Yet as a reaction against global standardization, the first decades of the twenty-first century also saw the rise of independent, local brands trying to define their difference and authenticity. From coffee packaging to craft beer, a local graphic identity, comprising packaging, promotional materials, and marketing, needs to convey the idea of small batches, hand-made processes, or some kind of craft or artisanal ideal. Using retro typography, illustration, and imagery, for example, might project an image of old-fashioned, community values and create a sense of tradition for new businesses.

Pushing this further, a product's packaging can be not only a visual representation of a company, but also their ethical stance (sustainability, fair trade, or locally made), source of materials, or geographical location. This way, a New Yorker or Londoner can distinguish between the Starbucks "mermaid" logo and that of a local, fair-trade café (although, ironically, the coffee beans of both originate in the same place). Such a graphic identity appeals to consumers wanting to show their allegiance to such values and meanings, so that design helps distinguish and communicate information about identities as much as products.

Visualizing data

Designers translate and structure a potentially overwhelming mass of facts and figures—data—into legible forms such as diagrams, maps, charts, and timetables. Such visual displays can be used to prove or disprove arguments, and help make data engaging or memorable. Organizing complexity, creating hierarchies, sifting through data to find the relevant pieces in order to make information clear and legible to non-specialists is a subtle art. As with other design fields, we know the failures all too well—excessive information, too much or not enough detail, poor ordering, poor use of space, hierarchies, colors, or line weights. Poor design can not only confuse but also convey the wrong ideas.

A specific form, data visualization, is the visual presentation of numeric values in charts, tables, or diagrams that transform raw numbers into clear visuals. From business to science, medicine to transportation, mapping data for various reasons is now a vital role for designers. Bubble charts on maps that indicate populations, for example, patterns of migration or disease, sports graphics that map shots taken on a basketball court, or the millions of tiny lines of Facebook's popular map of global connections, "Visualizing Friendships." Designers are increasingly working with data in various ways in order to clarify complexity and reveal new insights.

Early data visualizations included maps, scientific illustrations, and engineering diagrams. More modern visualizations began with William Playfair's graphs and charts in his 1786 book *The Commercial and Political Atlas*. Playfair, a Scottish engineer, writer, and draftsman, created visual charts for comparisons and overviews of statistical data on the English economy. Rather than just quoting numbers, Playfair believed charts and graphs convey information visually—so his readers could see trends, differences, and patterns quickly and clearly. His chart of the national debt of England, for example, clearly depicts the sharp rise in debt after the beginning of the American War. Although they had some political impact at the time, Playfair's innovations in visualizing data remained little known or used.

Later, others developed different types of visualizations: charts and diagrams that could not simply inform but actively persuade too. In 1858, for example, Florence Nightingale designed an innovative chart (technically, a polar chart but commonly known as a Nightingale chart) to depict the number of British soldiers who died by disease rather than in battle during each month of the Crimean War. Her "Diagram of the Causes of Mortality in the Army in the East" helped persuade the British parliament that bad hygiene, not battle wounds, was the major cause of death, and led to sanitation reform.

For the 1900 Paris Exposition, sociologist and activist W. E. B. Dubois, in collaboration with students from Atlanta University, created "The Exhibit of American Negroes." As well as photographs and maps, their exhibit included fifty-eight colorful charts that encapsulated Dubois's sociological research on African-American life in the South. Hand-painted in ink and watercolors, the charts and diagrams of economic and social statistics were powerful visualizations, intended by Dubois "to give, in as systematic and compact a form as possible, the history and present condition of a large group of human beings." Less than fifty years after the end of slavery, Dubois graphically presented African Americans' ongoing struggle for recognition and inclusion.

These examples of early data visualizations established the principles of later data and information design: each of these innovators realized that visual chunks of organized data are easier to recall, hierarchies help readers understand which data is most important, and visualizations help the audience establish relationships between various pieces of information. They also realized the persuasive power of such graphic visualization—otherwise abstract numbers or facts could be transformed into rhetorical images that could persuade an audience, and, particularly in the case of Dubois, make an otherwise invisible community visible.

Data visualization grew exponentially in the late twentieth century. In scientific research, textbooks, newspapers, technical manuals, and corporate reports, data visualization became essential for the communication of complex ideas. But some designers were critical of what the influential designer Edward Tufte referred to as "chartjunk," "cosmetic decoration, which frequently distorts the data ... who would trust a chart that looks like a video game?"[18] Tufte proposed an elegant, functional approach that opposed the more colorful, decorative, or whimsical approaches such as in Nigel Holmes' visualizations for *Time* magazine in the 1980s or those found in *USA Today*. But, such arguments against gimmicks and clichés risk losing audience engagement and general interest.

The idea of a universal, objective language of visualizing data has been around since the early twentieth century. In 1920s Vienna, Otto and Marie Neurath developed the "Vienna Method of Pictorial Statistics" to educate museum visitors. With German graphic designer Georg Arntz, they created ISOTYPE (International System of Typographic Picture Education) by using standard, modular units that could stand in for numbers. A simple vocabulary of silhouetted representations—a man, a woman, a plane—stood in for numerical units so that one plane, for example, represented 100 planes. Such symbols, the creators believed, could make complex statistical knowledge accessible and transcend linguistic and cultural boundaries. But, while the Neuraths believed in the social mission of their pictographic language, they inevitably had to compromise. "To remember simplified pictures," Otto Neurath wrote, "is better than to forget accurate numbers."[19]

Following Neurath's point, it is worth pausing to consider how the information we design today is organized, filtered, and analyzed, as well as how it is visually represented and disseminated. There is a danger in interpreting visualizations as objective or truthful representations of reality. All data visualizations are constructed—or designed—and need to be read critically. Every day, corporations, governments, and organizations use various forms of visualization to express quantitative analyses in legible formats. Clarity, precision, and fact are implied and can be persuasive, even if the data, its analysis, or the way it is designed, is flawed. Ideally, the viewer should be actively reading the content and contemplating the consequences, the relationships, or the patterns of any visualization.

Finally, data visualizations often appear scientific, impersonal and thus appear to represent an expert, neutral point of view. But, as Catherine D'Ignazio and Lauren F. Klein put it, all knowledge is "situated," that is, produced in "a particular social, cultural and material context," and all data is subject to inclusion and exclusion.[20] They urge us to ask questions of data visualizations, such as who collected the data, under what conditions, who funded the research, and who filtered and analyzed the raw data? They draw attention to the limits of such seemingly complete visual images, asking whose data is missing and who is empowered or disempowered by the visualization. D'Ignazio further suggests that we should be actively designing for our gaps in knowledge, making data collection more transparent and introducing public participation in interactive data visualization.

Finding our way

An airport, hospital, resort, sports stadium, college campus, or other large institutional complex can appear maze-like and intimidating for visitors. Wayfinding or environmental graphic design is the field devoted to developing clear orientation signs by which we can navigate such places. Like other fields of communication design discussed above, the combination of typography, colors, forms, and size is essential in creating a user-friendly navigation system, yet there are also overlaps with interior design, architecture, and urban planning. Signage may contain a combination of symbols, images, and/or text used on discrete signs, existing walls, or infrastructure. Arrows for direction, for example, pictograms to indicate bathrooms, regulatory signs warning us to Mind the Gap or Do Not Touch all help us navigate our physical environment.

Such signage systems vary from individual signs to complete network systems—for a train network, for example, or a highway system signage—designers need to create a consistent, concise, and clear scheme. Typically, design involves developing a sequence that begins with understanding how people will navigate a place, which paths and patterns people use, or how traffic circulates. But in an art gallery or museum, signage may need to do more than simply provide directions. Digital touch screens, for example, might aid further investigation by providing visitors with additional information. The balance between simplicity and complexity, clarity and stimulation, can be subtle. And, the bigger the design project, the more stakeholders that need to be involved.

In 2004, the Federal Highway Administration (FHWA) approved a new font, Clearview, for use on American highways. Clearview was designed to replace Highway Gothic, used since the 1940s, on 50,000 miles of highways. Its designers, Meeker and Associates, conducted extensive research into visibility, spacing, contrast, and weight of letters in order to make a font that was more legible than earlier fonts, particularly at night, in bad weather, and at a distance. But in 2016, the FHWA returned to the old font, claiming Clearview reduced legibility in signs with black letters on white or yellow fields (such as speed limit signs), and its better visibility could be due to the new signs. But an inconsistent patchwork of state and federal legislation, budget issues, and familiarity also affected the FHWA decision. Even with well-researched, thoughtfully designed systems standards are difficult to change, costly, and require widespread acceptance.

More successfully, Henry C. Beck's 1931 map of the London Underground (commonly known as the "Tube Map"), first used in 1933, is an icon of transportation graphics. Unlike a map, Beck's diagram had no relationship to topography or distance, and only the stylized Thames River provided a visual link to the landscape above. Its color-coded, simple lines created a modernist map in which space was compressed and stylized, with the geometric clarity of an electrical circuit board. Rather than trace the spaghetti lines of each route, Beck standardized all the angles to either 45 degrees or 90 degrees, codifying and abstracting the system. By focusing only on underground stations and the connections between them, Beck made a complex system more accessible.

But Beck's visualization had limitations. Distances between stations were not accurate and there was no distinction between one station and another (apart from diamond-shaped interchanges). The diagram was a simple network that implied a flow of people around the city from home to work to sites of leisure. The Tube Map enabled commuters and tourists to envisage a potentially confusing system of railway lines at a glance. And it was so successful that today, an updated version of Beck's diagram still appears in and around all Tube stations, on brochures, websites, and souvenirs.

But now, digital platforms are redefining transportation design and wayfinding. Rather than static diagrams like Beck's, interactive apps and customizable "personal travel assistants" available on smartphones are increasingly used by commuters and tourists. The London Tube Map app, for example, uses the original Beck design elements but adds real-time information such as service delays or changes, personal journey planning (with both cost and estimated time), GPS location, and additional information about places of interest near each station. The promise of future voice-controlled AI may offer both more dynamic data and a more personal (rather than universal, standardized) experience in the future.

Yet standardized systems still have a place. The organizing committee of the 1964 Tokyo Olympics realized that developing information signs in ninety different languages was impossible, so needed a universal symbolic language. Artistic director Masaru Katzumie and graphic designer Yoshiro Yamashita developed a system of simple pictograms to represent each sport, as well as information signs for the airport, transportation system, and sports venues, depicting services such as trains, first aid, bathrooms, and banks. Their system was influential for later designers of Olympic pictograms and signage. Global events such as the Olympic Games required symbols that were not reliant on national languages or particular cultural references and so a standardized, pictographic language continued to fill the brief in the late twentieth century.

Yet even such standard pictographic systems are subject to cultural nuances. More recently, the 2008 Beijing Olympics pictograms specifically referenced ancient Chinese seals and "Oracle Bone" characters so that the simple, stylized pictograms embodied centuries of Chinese culture as well as useful information. Such graphic systems are also connected to branding, so that, for example a sports stadium signage might be branded with team logos and colors in addition to directions. Or in historic districts, imagery and typography might evoke the past as well as map places of interest. In these cases, design functions not only to provide directions for visitors, but also in reinforcing the brand identification of a physical place by evoking a distinctive character.

CASE STUDY 2: INFOGRAPHICS

Typically composed of a mix of charts, maps, diagrams, illustrations, and/or text, infographics (an abbreviation of "information graphics") aim to clarify complex information in a visual form. They can be static or dynamic, narrative or sequential, but they are typically designed to not only inform but also engage. Infographics create a story to incite interest, explain, directly mobilize, or move a viewer—to educate, stimulate, or entertain. Like data visualizations, they display statistics or data to enable further analysis or explanation. Ideally, both provide the viewer with the tools to navigate and extract information. Used in various contexts, from annual reports to newspapers, scientific papers to marketing material, infographics might help explain how the brain works, map the solar system, or chart government spending.

This example (Figure 5) is composed of scenes arranged in a sequence that combine images, text, and figures. People appear in both silhouette (an employee and then a fire-fighter, distinguished by the firefighter's helmet, tank, and hose) in an elevation on the left and then a three-dimensional building, cut-away to reveal the interior on the right. Numbered and timed annotations alongside each scene help us follow the sequence of events, and on the far right, tiny icons—descendants of ISOTYPE—stand in for each truck and person involved in the action. Images,

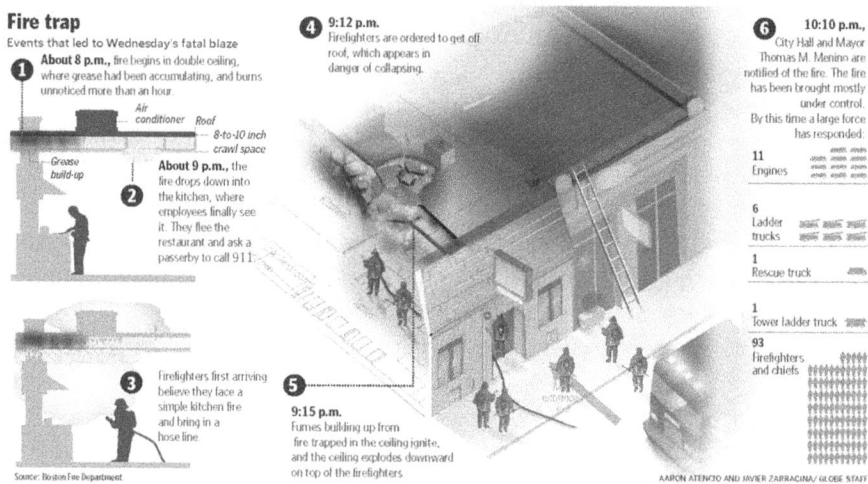

FIGURE 5 *Visual story and infographics of a fire, from the* Boston Globe, *2012. Getty Images: Graphic by Aaron Atencio and Javier Zarracina/The Boston Globe via Getty Images.*

words, and data are arranged to quickly make sense of the cause of the fire and the effort to put it out.

Previously confined to print media (such as newspapers and magazines), now digital infographics can be dynamic, animated, and interactive. They might include audio, virtual, or augmented reality to enhance the story. Animation has begun to replace traditional textbook diagrams, for example, to explain complex scientific theories, such as the structure of DNA or evolutionary theory. Interactive infographics allow users to actively select, search, or shape information, while web-based infographics provide real-time, changing data feeds.

Working with a graphic or interaction designer, a statistician, journalist, scientist, or sports analyst today can create interactive infographics that include personalized information generators such as calculators and "big data" visualizations where users can select, edit, or combine statistical data. But complexity and personalized options can go too far. For the BBC, for example, as part of their Global Experience Language, the ideal infographic is informative, engaging, and accessible.[21]

Ideally, infographics do not just communicate information but prompt further thought, research, and investigation. And, while such visualizations can educate, they can also profoundly mislead the viewer (intentionally or not), particularly when used in strategic communication, publicity, or for promotional purposes. As with all visualizations, a critical approach to reading is necessary.

The return to craft

In 1891, designer, author, and critic William Morris founded the Kelmscott Press in order to print books that had "a definite claim to beauty."[22] The mass-produced publishing of the time, believed Morris, had diluted not only book design but also the pleasure of reading. Although inspired by medieval calligraphy and illustration, Morris's reaction to the industrialization of publishing went beyond aesthetics, aiming to restore the workshop ideals and the value of craft in an era of mass production. His books—hand-printed on hand-made paper with hand-sewn bindings and woodcut illustrations—were not only a return to fine craft but also designed to be read slowly and treasured.

Perhaps, like Morris, the recent revival of retro typefaces and return of woodblock printing and metal type is a contemporary reaction against the standardization of our digital visual world. The logos, typefaces, and images used by companies such as Spotify, Pinterest, and Airbnb exemplify a new type of generic simplification, created for a global, mass audience. By the end of the 2010s, the new norm of corporate branding for tech companies comprised sans-serif type, black and white or flat colors, and abundant white space—based on ideals of simplicity, consistency, and clarity. This new corporate minimalism included no fun fonts, no hand lettering, or illustration. Designed to be universal, it was devoid of any personality.

In contrast, the hand-drawn lettering and expressive typefaces exemplified by the work of Erik Marinovich or Lauren Hom is not just driven by nostalgia for a pre-digital era. Mixing fonts and adding illustrative details, decorative flourishes, embossing or de-embossing, and hand-writing for advertising, branding, book covers, posters, signs, or murals also evoke distinction and individuality. If modern typography was a system of interchangeable letters, standardized and repeatable, lettering is a unique visual rendering of text, drawn by hand, unique, and personal. Vintage photographs, retro clip art, and quirky typography also evoke an imagined era when graphic design and life were supposedly simpler and somehow more authentic.

Ironically, this revival of hand-crafted methods and retro graphics is disseminated—perhaps even driven—by digital communication tools. Online platforms such as Etsy, Instagram, and Pinterest are the primary means for sharing, inspiration, and generating business for such graphic practices. The ideals and value of craft associated with early commercial artists and graphic designers have also led to a revival of interest in using pre-digital printing machines, hand-made paper, and hand-drawn illustrations. In contrast to the digitization of visual communication over the past two decades, this new maker culture around graphic media is devoted to originality, experimentation, and singularity that stand opposed to the predictable visual language of global corporate brands.

Yet there is also a part of this revival which is driven by a return to physical materials, particularly the tactile qualities of printed paper impressed with text, whether in the form of a book, card, or poster. Interestingly, some designers are mixing old and new processes in a conscious and innovative way. Type and information designer Erik Spiekermann's experimental studio, p98a in Berlin, for example, combines production on old printing presses, using metal and wood type with computers, laser cutters, and 3D printers to create a kind of "post-digital" approach to printing books, publications, and posters. Such mixes of digital and analog tools suggest the best of both worlds—the precision and repetition of the digital realm and the sensuous qualities of the material realm.

Chapter summary

- Designers create meaningful marks such as simple icons and logos
- Visual imagery communicates group and individual identities
- Data visualizations can inform, persuade, and promote
- Wayfinding helps us navigate our physical and digital environments
- Craft and physical making have reappeared in an increasingly digital world

2
Things

We know nothing about what the earliest humans said or thought, but we do know they made, used, and discarded things. We know Paleolithic people chipped and crafted stones to use as cutting blades, hammers, or spear heads. That is, we know they designed tools and weapons. While chimpanzees occasionally use sticks and stones as tools, they do not prototype or refine them. Only humans consciously *design* things. But early humans applied their inventive capacities to things other than tools and weapons. The remains of stone, bone, and shell ornaments indicate that Paleolithic people also valued material things as expressions of individual or group identity. That is, they designed not only useful things, but also things that embodied status or a sense of belonging.

Things are the objects, products, or artifacts we design and use, and, like things designed by our Paleolithic forebears, today's things are both functional and meaningful. More formally, design historian Judy Attfield described things as "objects of human production and exchange with and through which people live their everyday existence."[1] Our furniture, clothes, automobiles, electronic devices, as well as our houses, apartment blocks, and offices are designed things that enable us to live, work, play, and interact. Useful, beautiful, luxurious, or mundane, someone somewhere designed all of these things around us consciously and carefully. Or as we will see below, sometimes not so carefully.

A thing suggests an object separate from humans and from nature, an object we have consciously made that stands apart from us. But sometimes there are no such distinctions. A hip replacement or artificial limb, for example, becomes an integral part of our body, while our clothing and personal possessions help define our identity. An abandoned ship becomes a home for fish, while contemporary designers working with biomaterials are experimenting with shelters made from living fungi and lights powered by bacteria. In these cases, it is hard to distinguish between things designed by humans and natural phenomena. Keeping in mind such fuzzy boundaries, this chapter explores the complexities of designing, making, and consuming things.

From mechanization to automation

For millennia, people have employed standardization and repetition to produce things on a large scale, such as terracotta pots, bronze coins, and, as we saw in Chapter 1, books. But British industrialists radically changed manufacturing in the late eighteenth century. In his Soho Manufactory, Matthew Boulton used James Watt's steam-powered engine to mass-produce buckles, buttons, and silver-plated ornaments while Josiah Wedgwood's Etruria factory adopted the same engine to aid in producing ceramics. These new factories also systematized a division of labor that separated production into specialized activities. This included specialists who sketched or modeled prototypes, such as the artist John Flaxman, who designed vases and decorative details for Wedgwood. Despite these changes, product (or industrial) design was not yet a recognized profession.

A British Parliamentary Select Committee on Art and Manufactures, established in 1835, raised the status of designing mass-produced things. In response to falling exports and concern that British products were inferior to French and German products, the Committee's reports included recommendations on copyright legislation and specialist design education. British government participation over the next two decades included not only establishing Schools of Design but also public education through design exhibitions, lectures, and publications. An early graduate of the Schools, Christopher Dresser was perhaps the first professional industrial designer, and his studio produced sketches and models for mass-produced metalware, glassware, and ceramics in the 1870s and 1880s.

Meanwhile, American industrialists quickly adopted and improved mass-production processes. The so-called American system, developed in the early nineteenth century, was characterized by assembly line production, mechanization, and standardization. Samuel Colt's innovations in gun manufacturing, for example, included standardized, interchangeable parts designed to maximize production efficiency. Typically, American entrepreneurs or engineers (rather than specialist designers) designed mass-produced machines such as guns, sewing machines, typewriters, and bicycles, emphasizing functionality, affordability, and ease of manufacture.

One of the most successful, Henry Ford, applied these ideas to a more complex machine. Ford's "Model T" automobile first rolled off production lines in 1908. Affordable, durable, and flexible (early models were used as tractors as well as transport), the Model T soon became the most popular automobile in the United States. Ford's efficient assembly line and standardized parts increased productivity and lowered costs but limited consumer choice, as in Ford's playful quip to his sales representatives: "Any customer can have a car painted any color that he wants so long as it is black."[2] The Model T was, in fact, available in other colors, but Ford's point was that its design was so simple, functional, and efficient that such choices were unnecessary.

In response to Ford's success, Alfred P. Sloan, the head of General Motors, implemented annual model changes to encourage consumers to update their automobile. Within seven years, General Motors sales surpassed Ford, in part due to what critics called "planned obsolescence" in which a new design every year would make last year's model appear obsolete. A later champion of "planned obsolescence," industrial designer Brooks Stevens, believed the concept was central to a profession that aimed to incite consumers' "desire to own something a little newer, a little better, a little sooner than is necessary."[3] This is an idea that still sounds familiar today.

In one of the earliest books on the profession, designer Harold Van Doren defined the industrial designer's role as "to interpret the function of useful things in terms of appeal to the eye; to endow them with beauty of form and color; above all to create in the consumer the desire to possess."[4] Separating themselves from the engineers who made things work, the first American industrial designers in the 1920s and 1930s made mass-produced machines desirable. Sweeping curves on a streamlined surface suggested speed, efficiency, and progress, even on stationary things such as a lamp, radio, or desk. Closely aligned to advertising, marketing, and promotion, industrial design emerged as a kind of value-adding profession, mediating between machine manufacturing and the consumer marketplace.

But some European designers advocated an alternative approach. Modernists celebrated functional products designed for a mass society reshaped around new technology. Architect Le Corbusier famously described a house as a "machine for living" that contained not furniture, but equipment that "is no more than an extension of our limbs; its elements, in fact, *artificial limbs.*"[5] This modernist consensus of technological evolution toward a mechanized utopia promised a new future with a more significant role for designers. Yet the modernist mantra "form follows function" marginalized ornament, decoration, and color—good design was founded on universal principles, abstraction, and technological progress.

After the Second World War, new synthetic materials made possible by advances in chemistry changed the possibilities for designers. Plastics were malleable, lightweight, and flexible and proved useful in designing everything from children's toys to sewage pipes. Earl Tupper launched his Tupperware range of plastic storage containers and serving products in 1948, for example, bringing this new material into the heart of the American home. Plastic fibers, such as nylon and polyester, and new synthetic dyes offered a rainbow of colors and new fabrics for clothing and textiles. Plastic soon became the most widespread material created by humans and promised almost infinite possibilities for designing things.

As mass production increased, a crucial problem facing manufacturers was that in order to maximize economies of scale, they could only offer minimal product diversity. Factories and machine tools were expensive, and redesigning things was slow and difficult. Led by Toyota, Japanese auto manufacturers developed the "just-in-time" system in the 1950s and 1960s, which used the same machinery for different models or components, mixed schedules for assembly lines, and used subsidiaries and subcontractors for parts. The increased flexibility allowed for more variations and options for finished autos as well as incremental improvements. As manufacturers applied these processes to other industries, change cycles accelerated to allow even faster obsolescence.

In the 1980s and 1990s, the introduction of Computer-Aided Design (CAD) software fundamentally changed industrial and product design. CAD enabled designers to visualize new products with great precision, and to modify, refine, and edit their designs on screen. Accurate and flexible, as well as mapping a three-dimensional product, CAD software was capable of storing additional data, such as material variations or tolerances. The gradual replacement of manual sketching, drafting, and documentation redefined how designers envisaged three-dimensional things.

Combined with CAD, Computer Aided Manufacturing created a powerful means to produce things. To automate manufacturing, CAD models are sent directly to computer-driven machines and robots. While automotive and electronics manufacturers began using industrial robots as early as the 1960s, the gradual increase in automation affected most mass-produced things by the turn of the twenty-first century. Combined with offshore production in the late twentieth century, the separation of design from the increasingly automated production process seemed almost complete.

But another new process, 3D printing, may reverse this trend. Rather than casting or molding, 3D printing is an additive process, laying down thin layers of a material to form a solid object. Initially used in the aerospace and automotive industries to create specialized parts, it was soon adapted to medical, fashion, and product applications. At first, only plastics and metals were printed but now 3D printers can use a range of materials, including biomaterials. In the last decade, the gradual reduction in price of desktop 3D printers has made rapid prototyping affordable and facilitated the design and production of customizable things, at least on a small scale.

Serial things

"Designed by Apple in California. Assembled in China." This statement, printed on the back of Apple products, is a brief account of a complex process. The iPhone X, for example, contains components made and designed in South Korea, Japan, and Taiwan. Its raw materials include aluminum for the case, silicon for the microchip and dozens of rarer materials—cobalt from the Congo, tin from the Philippines, rare earth materials from Inner Mongolia, and lithium from Bolivia. Similarly, German-designed BMWs and Japanese-designed Toyotas are assembled in the United States from parts manufactured all over the world and raw materials drawn from similarly diverse places. Compared to Ford's era, contemporary design, manufacture, and distribution are global and complex.

The designer's role in creating mass-produced things is also complex. A design brief—whether developing a new thing or updating an old one—involves numerous choices. In choosing one form, color, or material over another, designers make choices that reflect not only functional values (will the product work as intended? is it easy to use? is it safe?) but also economic (is it cost-effective?), cultural (is it understandable?), and environmental (is it sustainable?) values. At almost every stage of the design process, alternative solutions abound, and designers ideally try to find the best possible.

In applying a sleek, shiny surface to a train or radio so it looked efficient, progressive, and futuristic, early industrial designers understood the communicative value of things. The clean surfaces of streamlined products, for example, appeared hygienic and confirmed the mid-century American ideals of cleanliness, while their futuristic forms suggested a technologically advanced society. Although dismissed by some designers as styling or surface decoration, professional product designers must still engage with the language of forms. Things elicit emotional responses.

We recognize common forms and learn the visual vocabulary of things. We value the sustainability of an unbleached linen bag, smile at a quirky kettle, or covet the luxurious folds of silk. Designers have long tried to use this language to embed social or cultural meanings into the forms of mass-produced things. The study of sign systems, or semiotics, is based on the idea that all manufactured things are signs that communicate ideas. They do this in literal or in metaphoric ways. The language of products is not only visual, as other senses also express meaning to users. Touch, for example, and our non-physical interaction with things such as desire or memories also affect how we interact with things.

In the 1950s, French literary critic Roland Barthes argued that mass-produced things had become so distanced from their producers, production process, and materials that they appeared to consumers to be conjured up by magic. Mediated via glossy color advertisements, everyday things were not just functional tools, but enchanting commodities saturated with latent meaning. The new Citroën D.S. automobile, Barthes explained, was more than a useful mode of transport. Its design, promotion, and reception in the French popular imagination inaugurated an era in which automobiles are "consumed in image if not in usage by an entire population which appropriates them as a purely magical object."[6]

Barthes used the term "myth" in his analysis of such "magical" commodities to reveal that, even in the sophisticated modern culture of post-war France, things expressed collective values. Individuals assimilate—consciously or unconsciously—the symbolic languages, ideologies, or conventions within which products appear. For Barthes, everyday things operate as elements in a system of communication governed by rules and relations that appear timeless and universal, submerging their historical and contingent nature. Of course, over the next fifty years, the rise of advertising, branding, and promotional strategies made it harder and harder to divorce things from their mythical status.

Apple products' distinctive aesthetic, for example, comprises refined forms that avoid decorative or ornamental detail, reductive colors, and a precision and harmony that not only make a complex machine appear simple to use but also express ideals about the company's philosophy. The aesthetic purity, soft curves, and futuristic form of the iPhone's aluminum case, for example, even as it is redesigned and upgraded almost every year, retain a formal consistency. This coherent vocabulary of forms and materials then becomes an expectation of consumers and an essential element in a coherent branding and advertising campaign.

Some design consultants develop signature styles that they apply to everyday objects, creating their own distinctive visual vocabulary. Through the 1990s and 2000s, Karim Rashid's dayglo-colored plastic, Naoto Fukasawa's modest minimal or Philippe Starck's quirky, poetic furniture and homeware collections, all became recognizable signature styles. Starck and Rashid extended their furniture into interiors for restaurants, hotels and apartments to create all-encompassing lifestyle brands embodied in their designer things. In a different way, the Dutch collective Droog Design developed furniture and homewares as condensed concepts that challenge users to think. Using irony, their repurposed, recycled, and playful objects provoke critiques of consumerism and waste. Both cases illustrate how people interact with everyday things not only in functional terms, but emotionally and mentally.

Extending this idea further, anthropologists have usefully proposed that things have "biographies" whose meanings change over time.[7] The meaning of blue denim jeans, for example, was originally working class and male. Levi Strauss's original industrial clothing—inexpensive, durable, and practical—was associated with laboring men. In Hollywood films, particularly in the 1940s and 1950s, blue jeans came to be associated with cowboys, rebels, and outsiders. Their popularity spread with youth subcultures and jeans eventually became mainstream. Now, blue denim jeans are a global fashion staple, with a range from luxurious to everyday styles, for men, women, and children. Over a long period such as this, the cultural and social meanings associated with blue denim jeans have clearly changed, and designers respond to these changes.

As well as understanding such changing meanings, designing things for people involves creating products that fit people's needs and are safe to use. Ergonomics is the process of designing spaces, products, and systems to fit with human bodies and the way they work. Initially developed by the military after the Second World War in order to address problems with standardization in cockpit design, designers later applied ergonomic principles to factories, workplaces, and products. While cost effective and efficient, standardization reduces individual users to average users. And there is no such person as an average user. Researchers into ergonomics have developed an entire science devoted to ideal chairs, desks, and office tools based on not only the differing physical aspects of humans such as size, weight, and reach, but our psychological variety too.

Given the differences in height, weight, and body types, even a seemingly simple thing like a chair is not easy to design. Designers Bill Stumpf and Don Chadwick, originally hired by Herman Miller to design furniture for the elderly, took up the challenge to design an ergonomic office chair that could fit a wide range of bodies. The resulting chair, the Aeron, comprised a molded plastic frame and a mesh of woven plastic fibers pulled taut for a backrest. Mechanical levers adjusted the height and back position, and the mesh molded to accommodate various body types. Such was the designer's attention to efficiency that this was an office chair reduced to essentials, a chair constructed from partially recycled materials and designed for easy disassembly and recycling.

Launched in 1994, the Aeron chair quickly became an icon in new tech companies, and continued to be a best-seller for the next two decades. The engineered look, materials, and adjustable levels of support proved so popular that Herman Miller launched a redesigned version with new materials and ergonomic tweaks in 2016. But, with increased attention on workplace wellness and the acknowledgment that excess sitting causes back and neck pain, perhaps even the most ergonomic chair is not the only solution to furnishing an office. Many contemporary offices offer varied options, including adjustable desks to allow for standing or sitting, as well as programs to encourage mobility. In this sense, no chair at all may be the most ergonomic office solution!

A crucial problem is that ergonomic guidelines are inherently based on averages rather than individuals. But standardization is both a constraint and a necessity for designers. Building codes, for example, restrict certain materials, forms, or sizes for reasons of safety, quality control, usability, or environmental protection. In product design also, standards can take various forms, from informal standards such as company guidelines about a product range to standards codified nationally or internationally by industries, certification organizations, trade associations, or governments. Ideally, these standards should respond to past failures and current ergonomic research. For consumers, standardization is also not necessarily a bad thing, particularly when it mandates accessibility, health and safety, environmental regulations, consistency, and compatibility.

Yet even within such standard guidelines, designers need to identify potential health and safety issues to minimize potential risks. Defective design claims can result in legal liability and physical harm. When Samsung's Galaxy Note 7 smartphones started exploding in 2016, for example, the company recalled 2.5 million of them. Blamed on a manufacturing error in the lithium-ion batteries, the explosions apparently had nothing to do with the device's design. But, if consumers could have simply replaced the faulty batteries, there would be no need to recall the phones. In imitation of Apple's phones, designers of the Samsung cases created a seamless case by completely sealing it, making repair impossible. As with many contemporary electronics, designing for repair is not part of the brief. These magical things are not only designed to appear from nowhere, but are destined to disappear from our lives onto a mountain of e-waste in some distant place.

CASE STUDY 3: CHAIRS

In 2015, industrial designer Marc Newson's "Lockheed Lounge" sold at auction for £2,434,500 (just over US $3 million), a record price for a single piece of furniture by a living designer. One of a limited edition of 10 developed by Newson in 1988, each lounge was hand-crafted from fiberglass-reinforced polyester resin covered by a patchwork of aluminum panels. The streamlined metallic form suggested an aircraft's body, as did its name. The Lounge shot to fame when Madonna reclined on one in her video for the 1993 song, Rain. Although never destined for mass production, the Lockheed Lounge's materials and form clearly appealed to a certain audience.

Another Newson chair, the "Doha Lounge Chair" (Figure 6) had a similarly distinctive name and a now-famous creator. Such furniture is bought and sold

FIGURE 6 *Marc Newson's "Doha Lounge Chair," a 2012 prototype, sold at auction in 2015 for £27,500 ($35,000 US). Getty Images: Credit: Tristan Fewings/ Stringer.*

in art galleries, in designer furniture stores, and at international auction houses. The designer's intention is clearly not to create a comfortable support to watch television but a sculptural object to admire. In this case, designer furniture approaches art, its purpose is contemplation rather than function, and aesthetics in a narrow sense of looking but not touching. This is not to disparage Newson's contributions to design, but unfortunately such designer furniture continues to inform public perceptions about industrial design, situating it alongside style, taste, and luxury.

In contrast, the molded plastic chair, or monobloc, is probably the world's most popular piece of furniture. Available in US stores as the "plastic patio chair," it retails for as little as $10 (Figure 7). In the 1960s, designers such as Verner Panton, Robin Day, and Vico Magistretti experimented with new plastics to mass produce chairs. The most successful, Day's injection-molded polypropylene chair, a lightweight plastic shell atop slim aluminum legs, was mass produced in millions. By 1972, French engineer Henry Massonet devised a cost-effective, injection-molded chair completely made of plastic (a "monobloc") that could be produced in a factory in less than two minutes. Over the next fifty years, the technology spread and now plastic monobloc chair numbers could be in the billions.

Accessible and cheap, the monobloc has transcended cultures and spread globally. Although more functional than Newson's designer furniture, the monobloc's spread raises worrying questions about sustainability. Not only with its materials, but also in its affordability, the monobloc encourages disposability, particularly given many versions are not designed to last. Although situated at the extreme limits of affordability, neither Newson's chairs nor the monobloc chairs were designed with ergonomics in mind, their standardized forms are unlikely to suit all body types, and each assumes a singular way of sitting. Oddly, although finding something to sit on is no longer a problem, designers and architects continue to redesign the chair.

FIGURE 7 *A man sits by stacks of white and red monobloc chairs, Yangon, Myanmar, 2016. Getty Images: photo by Tessa Bunney/In Pictures via Getty Images.*

Singular things

Standardized mass production represents only one aspect of our world of things. From hand-crafted jewelry to the Sydney Opera House, we still value singular things. The boundaries between design, craft, and art have never been entirely clear, yet for a long time, mass-produced things seemed distinct from singular things. Industrial design seemed opposed to craft. Now, designing customized or personalized things is easier with new technologies, processes, and applications. From medical devices designed to fit individual bodies to personalized versions of popular shoes, variations along this spectrum between serial and singular things abound.

As we saw in Chapter 1, a revival of hand-crafted things in the last two decades has affected design, particularly in highly industrialized economies. Perhaps as a reaction to the standardized, global mass production of things, the rise of things designed and made by hand by an individual that we know (if only virtually) may reconnect design and production. A visible instance of this is "Indie craft," a broad movement that began to coalesce with the launch of Etsy in 2005. An online forum where makers can interact with customers to distribute their original art and craft products, Etsy enabled a revival of the hand-made economy via digital means. And not only through online forums and blogs but also in physical galleries and craft fairs, indie craft was driven as much by social ideals of creativity, DIY, and sustainable lifestyles as reactions against standardized mass production.[8]

A related development is the "maker movement" that emerged after the foundation of *MAKER* magazine in 2005. The magazine's focus on DIY integrates woodworking and metalworking with electronics, robotics, and digital fabrication. With the availability of tools such as 3D printers and the rise of makerspaces, fab labs (fabrication laboratories), and micro-factories, designers could potentially produce small batches or customized products. A generation ago, to become a craft practitioner required an apprenticeship in woodworking or metalwork, while now almost anyone can design something on computer for robots to manufacture. The promotion of maker culture in the 2010s included the promise of returning manufacturing to Europe and the United States as well as reconnecting design with making. Perhaps, rather than rely on mass-manufactured things made abroad, makers could design and create on a small scale, customizing and personalizing our everyday products.

Like crafters, makers emphasize the community aspect of sharing knowledge and skills within a physical space dedicated not only to making but also to education, inspiration, and collaboration. But contemporary maker culture is not as open and accessible as some promotors claim. American makerspaces, for example, were characterized by one researcher as "largely male, largely white, largely with tertiary education."[9] Craft's image as a female activity and making as a male activity are also long-standing stereotypes that seem embedded in these contemporary practices. Ultimately, both are primarily leisure activities rather than a means to paid work, and rarely focus on solutions to social or economic problems. And, in perhaps a sign of reappraisal of the promises of maker culture, the best-known makerspace franchise in the United States, TechShop, closed in 2018.

But both indie craft and maker culture underlined the idea that we are all potential designers. Their common interest in recycling, improvising, modifying, and redesigning also intersects with another recent phenomenon, "hacking." Originally a term taken from the computer industry, hacking is now applied to consumer products and other aspects of everyday life. In IKEA hacking, for example, consumers buy furniture from IKEA and modify, customize, repurpose, or personalize it then share their designs online via blogs or forums. IKEA hacking has proven so popular that in 2018, IKEA launched their own Tom Dixon-designed "Delaktig" modular living platform, specifically designed to accommodate "hacks." Grooves along the aluminum structure allow users to attach a side table, or magazine rack, and customers can convert it into a sleeping, work, or lounge space.

Such movements seem to have inaugurated a new era of consumption and participation. No longer will our futures contain standardized, mass-produced things designed elsewhere, but personalized, locally made, and individual things. On the one hand, there is an element of subversive political intervention and the promise of a material democracy, but on the other, such movements are also boosted as disruptive innovation and entrepreneurial business opportunities. But for all the DIY and supposed sustainability of indie craft and maker culture, both rely on global components, tools, and raw materials sourced elsewhere, as well as a global digital infrastructure for distribution.

While hacking is tolerated, or even glorified if it is done on a small scale with little economic or political effect, the unregulated mass copying of things is not. In the last two decades, China has become not only the so-called factory of the world, where much mass production takes place, but also home to pirating on a mass scale. Beginning in the 1980s in China's southern city of Shenzhen, many official factories manufactured high-tech products and fashion designed in Europe, the United States, or Japan. As well as official production, a local culture of copying expensive foreign products, including "designer" fashion and DVD, CD, and MP3 players, began at this time. Distribution was initially small scale and local, but spread to other Chinese cities and Chinatowns around the world.

In 2008, China's news media officially acknowledged the phenomenon known as *Shanzhai*. Translated as "mountain stronghold," *Shanzhai* conjured up images of bandits outside of official authority, but quickly became shorthand for "fake" or "imitation" products and the culture that spawned them.[10] In Shenzhen and surrounding cities around the Pearl River Delta, tiny *Shanzhai* workshops with specialization in manufacturing, design, software, and electronic engineering were producing imitations of Apple, Nokia, and Samsung phones and other electronic devices. With little financial capital, *Shanzhai* workshops utilized local expertise, machinery, and lax intellectual property laws to produce imitations of the latest phones, watches, and drones. Importantly, these replicas were sold at a fraction of the cost of the "real" brands.

By this time, China produced over 60 percent of the world's 1.2 billion cellphones manufactured every year. Shadowing this "official" production, *Shanzhai* producers began to modify the design of foreign phones to suit local conditions and new markets. This included, for example, designing phones with longer-life batteries, larger buttons, enhanced speakers and cameras, dual operating systems, or dual SIM card slots. *Shanzhai* designers could mix and match features from phones designed by Samsung or Apple to create an "enhanced" version that sold for less than half the price. Some *Shanzhai* phones were not simply imitations but improvements upon the original designs. In 2009, more than 200,000 people in the Pearl River Delta were producing millions of *shanzhai* phones, and suppling 20 to 30 percent of the Chinese market.[11] With internet distribution, production increased as *Shanzhai* phones are now exported to Africa and South America.

While many still regard China as the world's factory, *Shanzhai* suggests a rapidly growing culture of innovation. The subversion and creation of *Shanzhai* is similar to IKEA hacking, only on a much larger scale. But, the "bandit" character of *Shanzhai* design and production flaunted global intellectual property regulations, state certification, and tax laws, as well as environmental and safety standards. Yet copying has always been central to mass production—repetitive, exact copies are at the heart of the process. For Western designers and corporations, international copyright laws highlight originality and authenticity and they continue to value originality and authenticity in design (such as Newson's chair) even with mass-produced things. The Chinese tradition has no such cult of originality but a modular approach to technology, not founded on a proprietary model but instead on the idea that variations produce innovation.

Materials

In 2003, while sailing from Hawaii to California, Captain Charles Moore noticed plastic in the ocean around his ship. Not just a few scraps, but miles and miles of plastic debris. The subsequent media attention focused on what scientists have called the Great Pacific Trash Vortex (or Great Pacific Garbage Patch), a soupy collection of 80,000 tons of plastic waste in the North Pacific covering an area larger than Texas. Composed of microplastic particles, fishing material, plastic bottles, and fragments of mass-produced things, it is the result of pollution washed by marine currents and eddying around a single location. Although vast and spectacular, the Great Pacific Trash Vortex is only a fraction of the plastic waste that reaches landfills, backyards, and trash heaps.

The Trash Vortex is a vivid illustration of the unsustainability of our material culture. Ours is a throwaway culture founded on disposable things—single use plastic bottles, containers and packaging, fast fashion, and the planned obsolescence of smartphones, furniture, and automobiles. Designed for short-term use, then discarded for the next model, it seems unthinkable to consider using and reusing any one of these things for a lifetime. In environmental terms, the worst aspect of this phenomenon are plastics that are both dependent on fossil fuels and do not biodegrade. From Lego bricks to bottle caps, plastic is an incredibly flexible material to design things with, but its continued use means the Trash Vortex is only likely to get bigger.

Attention to the material properties of things has long been of interest to designers. Architect William McDonough and chemist Michael Braungart's influential book *Cradle to Cradle: Remaking the Way We Make Things*, for example, proposed a design method founded on natural processes. "This cyclical, cradle-to-cradle biological system," they argued, "has nourished a planet of thriving, diverse abundance for millions of years."[12] Modern industrial culture, based on cradle to grave design in which throwaway products are destined for landfill, could be countered by the principle of waste elimination. For McDonough and Braungart: "*To eliminate the concept of waste means to design things—products, packaging, and systems—from the very beginning on the understanding that waste does not exist.*"

From furniture made from plastic bottles or recycled paper pulp, the idea of reusing the materials of existing things as new things is a promising one that designers return to as one solution. But the reuse of materials to make new things only goes so far. There are, for example, limits to plastic recycling so that some plastics cannot be recycled or some only once. To extract the recyclable material from a complex machine may be incredibly time-consuming, expensive, or dangerous. So, taking the biological ideas of McDonough and Braungart further, designers are beginning to experiment with alternative, biodegradable materials such as luminescent bacteria to produce household lighting, or fungus-based materials to create furniture. Working with chemists and biologists, the cutting-edge of biomaterials suggests that alternatives to plastics are possible.

In 2017, Adidas, in partnership with Parley for the Oceans, designed and manufactured over 1 million sports shoes from ocean plastic debris.

While this represents a start, it is only part of a long-term strategy by the company to phase out plastic from production altogether. The first step is stop using virgin plastics and use recycled plastics. The next is to start using renewable, bio-materials. A recent experimental prototype is a shoe made from spider silk. After roughly two years of wear, the shoe can be composted in a suburban garden. Materials of the future, such as spider silk, yeast cells, algae and bacteria, are cultivated in a lab using living cells in a process called biofabrication.

Along similar lines, architect and designer Neri Oxman's Mediated Matter Group at MIT combines designers working with digital fabrication, chemistry, and biology. Like McDonough and Braungart, she argues that previously, designers rarely considered things in terms of their broader ecological impact. That is, they rarely questioned where raw materials come from and what happens after their intended use is finished. In response, Oxman proposes digitally engineered yet biologically informed products and buildings based on a theory of *growing* rather than manufacturing or assembling things—a process she refers to as "biologically engineered" design.[13] Through using computational design, materials engineering, synthetic biology, and additive manufacturing, designers such as Oxman are ultimately aiming for materials that operate within a self-replicating system. Future designers may look to silkworms to weave us shelters or compose cellphones from shellfish protein.

One of the promises of the early decades of the digital era was dematerialization—a shift away from our dependence on physical materials as we operated more and more in the virtual world. In some respects, this has happened as, for example, many people now pay bills online or access instruction manuals and information online rather than in printed physical formats. But in other respects, dematerialization has not played out as prophesized. Digital e-readers, for example, that potentially contain over a thousand books and magazines, were supposed to replace material books and magazines. After its launch in 2007, Kindle's e-book reader had mixed results, as e-books were not substantially cheaper nor screen-based reading as popular as first predicted.

A decade later, statistics for the UK showed a decline in e-book sales and a rise in print, with e-books claiming only 25–30 percent of the market.[14] A number of reasons might explain these figures, including the fact that consumers have larger phones and tablets so that a specialized e-reader is no longer a great advantage. Another is screen fatigue—given people are already spending a lot of time on screens—a material book may be a more enjoyable reading experience. Additionally, digital printing, online sales, and global shipping made print books even cheaper. Physical books, despite their reported demise, have not completely vanished.

While this is only one example, we clearly have not yet designed ourselves a virtual world that uses minimal physical resources. In fact, despite considerable changes due to digitization and networked technologies, we still inhabit an overwhelmingly material world, composed of materials most people know little about. Designing physical things remains a challenging task, and increasingly designers are thinking not only about where materials come from but also how to create things without using more raw materials. Solutions involving using existing materials, recycling, repairing, reusing, and sharing things are becoming part of standard design practice. Questioning the broader ecological impact of materials is also becoming a central concern of industrial and product design practice and education.

CASE STUDY 4: KICKSTART MONEYMAKER PUMP

The American founders of design and development company KickStart, Martin Fisher, and Nick Moon set themselves a particularly difficult challenge: to design something that could change the lives of poor Kenyan farmers. The resulting product, which has proved instrumental in creating wealth, improving health, and developing businesses in sub-Saharan Africa, is a water pump.

Fisher and Moon began working in Kenya in the mid-1980s. Disillusioned with the dependence on overseas aid and gifts, they also had first-hand experience of design's failings in Africa. Although well-intentioned, Western designers usually resorted to a universal solution regardless of local needs or context. The resulting products were either too expensive or, if locally produced, of poor quality. And giving away products, usually intended for communal rather than individual ownership, meant that no one took responsibility for them.

With the entrepreneurial individual rather than the "poor victim" in mind, Fisher and Moon founded a non-profit in 1991 to design products and create a profitable business model. After designing low-cost pit latrines and a brick press, they noticed that subsistence farmers in Kenya were relying on seasonal rainfall and carrying buckets of water from wells to irrigate their crops.

The original MoneyMaker, launched in 1996, was a treadle-operated metal pump that could pull water up to seven meters from a well to an adjacent field. The next iteration, the Super MoneyMaker, had both this suction capability plus a pressure capability to push water through a pipe and spray it across two acres. With such an irrigation tool, a subsistence farmer with a small plot could grow crops all year round, expand production, and sell surplus crops.

The design requirements were daunting. The pumps needed to be durable, functional, and mass produced yet also portable, easily repairable, and culturally acceptable. And, to avoid the dependency trap, they had to be sold, but at a very low cost. Designed in Nairobi and initially manufactured locally, larger production facilities and lower costs in China eventually shifted much of KickStart's production offshore. Even so, at US $95 for a large treadle pump, or even $35 for a less powerful hand-operated version, the MoneyMaker is a significant—but worthwhile—investment for an African farmer.

But increasing agricultural income is only part of KickStart's aim. Establishing a profitable supply chain in which distributors and retailers also profit by selling pumps is another, and this too has proven sustainable. Although ideally aiming for a completely self-sufficient market, KickStart still relies on grants to subsidize marketing and development of new products.

As of April 2018, KickStart has sold over 300,000 pumps in sub-Saharan and West Africa, resulting in over 220,000 new businesses being created along the supply chain. Most importantly, these relatively simple designed products have reportedly lifted over a million people out of extreme poverty.

Ethics

In his 1971 classic *Design for the Real World: Human Ecology and Social Change*, designer Victor Papanek chastised Western designers for focusing their efforts solely on superficial products for wealthy consumers. An exhibition at New York's Cooper-Hewitt Design Museum in 2007, *Design for the Other 90%*, revisited these issues. While the exhibition suggested that little had changed in the design industry in over thirty years, it also encapsulated a new wave of design thinking. The exhibition's premise was challenging: "Ninety-five percent of the world's designers focus all of their efforts on developing products and services exclusively for the richest ten percent of the world's customers."[15] Like Papanek, many of the designers involved advocated designing low-cost, small-scale, locally made products for the "other 90%," rather than simply exporting mass-produced things that were designed and manufactured elsewhere.

Design for people without economic opportunities or those in environments whose needs are not being met—and not necessarily only in poor countries—has again become a central concern for designers. But the thinking on design for people in developing countries has shifted in two significant ways. First, designers have moved away from designing physical things to designing systems and services, particularly in areas such as healthcare, education, and government (these issues will be addressed in later chapters). Human-centered design approaches propose that what people need is usually not simply a new product but also one integrated into broader social, economic, and environmental systems (see Case Study 4). More importantly, designers in developed countries have realized that they need to collaborate with local designers, users, and authorities in order to design appropriate and sustainable solutions.

Meanwhile, even among the wealthy 10 percent, designers have also come to terms with the inherent assumptions and stereotypes built into the design of mass-produced things. Beginning in the 1980s and 1990s, feminist critics such as Penny Sparke and Pat Kirkham graphically illustrated not only the gender stereotypes embedded within certain designed things, but also the theoretical assumptions about the feminine "preoccupation with surface rather than substance, with ephemerality rather than universality, with appearance rather than with utility, and with the inessential rather than the essential."[16] Within twentieth-century design theory and practice, such assumptions about users often remained lurking below the surface, affecting the design of varied things. In our century, the way we design things still embodies social and cultural ideals, at times continuing longstanding clichés.

Children's toys, for example, have long been an area notable for gendered products, and, despite various critiques, stereotypes remain. The "coding" of things as male or female can be superficial, from cultural associations with particular colors (a pink scooter for girls, a silver one for boys), or on a more stereotypical level such as girls dress-up costumes as princesses or nurses, boys as superheroes or scientists. Occasionally, these gender stereotypes still appear in adult products such as women's fashionable headphones or man-sized tissues. In 2011, pen manufacture Bic launched a "Bic for Her" line of pens (comprising slim cases in a range of pastel colors), marketed as a "sleek pen silhouette" with "jeweled accents." Although the pens launched a social media frenzy and plenty of humorous reviews, they continued to be produced.

Gillette's long-standing Mach 3 and Venus disposable razors for men and women, respectively, are also still designed along gender stereotypes. The men's silver, blue, and black Mach 3 razor appears to be a highly efficient, engineered machine (and the name confirms an association with speed and machinery). In contrast, the curved forms of the women's Venus, in white, pale pink or purple colors, carefully conceal the blades. The Venus razor appears to be a magic wand delivered by the goddess to wave over the skin. These distinctions are reinforced by the razors' respective packaging, typography, and advertising. The same company, the same steel blades, yet the plastic forms, colors, and branding of each razor both draw upon and reinforce traditional stereotypes.

This is one aspect of how design and gender are related. Another, no doubt exacerbated by the fact that industrial design and engineering have been traditionally male domains, the large realm of products are designed—unintentionally perhaps—for male bodies. The statistical averages and ergonomic standards noted above have traditionally taken the average male body as the default size. But the average woman, for example, is shorter and weighs less than the average man. The male-centered design of products subsequently results in women (and children) perceived as the wrong size or creators of errors. The world's first artificial heart, for example, successfully transplanted in 2013, was designed with dimensions that fit 86 percent of men, but only about 20 percent of women.[17] In this case, the average male body is still the default.

But women are not the only ones affected by assumptions and stereotypes in the design of things and the material world. In the 1970s, Patricia Moore, a young designer working at Raymond Loewy's design consultancy, became frustrated by the lack of attention paid to elderly consumers. So, starting in 1979, she began a project in which she dressed as an elderly woman, with shoes that made walking difficult, glasses that impaired her vision, and ear plugs that impaired her hearing. She traveled to various American cities in wheelchairs and with a cane in order to try and experience life as an eighty-year-old woman. As a result of these experiences, Moore established her own design firm dedicated to designing better products for the elderly.

Developed via a role-play, Moore's "empathic model" provided her with "the first-hand experience that individuals face when they are made unable, by design."[18] Moore concluded that it is not an individual who is disabled, but it is their interactions with the designed world around them that make them disabled. Designers, she discovered, often assume generic levels of mobility, sensory ability, and motor skills of end users. Highlighting the failure of many designers to account for the broad range of users and abilities, Moore argues that designers should rethink everyday things with the aim of achieving "the universal possibilities of inclusion by design." The ongoing project of "universal design," which we will address in Chapter 5, is dedicated to this ideal.

Conclusion

Despite promises of a dematerialized culture, the design, production, and consumption of things rose exponentially in the early twenty-first century. Contrary to popular characterizations of a post-industrial society, our digital age has added more materials. The success of mass-production techniques and design for mass audiences has resulted in an overflow of things, particularly in wealthier countries where basic needs are largely met. Despite the sheer number of things around us, some designers continue to design and redesign chairs, lamps, or water bottles in new forms, colors, or materials, sustaining design's role in stimulating desire and obsolescence. But new ways of thinking about our relationships with things, explored in the next two chapters, suggest alternatives to the current situation.

Chapter summary

- Designing mass-produced things is a complex, global process
- Standardization brings both benefits and limitations for design
- New processes and materials offer alternatives to mass-produced things
- Designed things are embedded with cultural and social meaning
- Designed things can be inclusive and exclusive

3

Interaction

Computers, smart phones, touch screen interfaces, and software all require designing for use by people, and, with the increasing sophistication of AI and the Internet of Things, new types of devices need designing. In the past three decades, specialized fields such as Human–Computer Interaction (HCI) and Interaction Design have evolved as a response to the perceived shortcomings of an engineering paradigm which paid too much attention to machines and too little attention to their users. Today, designing for interaction facilitates the relationship not only between humans and new technological devices but also between humans and networked systems, and humans and robots, leading to new fields such as Human-Robot Interaction (HRI).

Designers have long contemplated products from the perspective of interaction. That is, they have always contemplated creating simpler, better tools and machines for humans to use. Interaction was always central to industrial, product, and graphic design, even if it was developed intuitively and improved gradually over a long period of time. Driving an automobile, for example, involves a series of interactions, some of which have changed very little over the past century while others have changed incrementally. We still push pedals for acceleration and braking, but increasingly, new automobiles include automated processes for headlights and windscreen wipers, as well as interactive screens for navigation, communication, and entertainment.

In this chapter, we will start by considering how an interactive design perspective applies to relatively simple products and machines. Then, we will examine how designers have contributed to our interactions with new technologies developed over the past two or three decades, including digital interfaces, software, and robots. Not surprisingly, interaction design is a field of considerable overlap, collaboration, and complexity. It draws upon communication and industrial design, but it is fundamentally interdisciplinary, connecting designers to hardware and software engineers as well as allied research from psychologists, linguists, and anthropologists.

Designing machines for people

Although humans have long improved the design of things to suit various uses and users, there was little concerted effort devoted to human-machine interaction until after the Second World War. Prior to this, trial and error typically decided the best way humans might interact with new machines. Standardization and uniformity were the accepted norms in designing the modern, mass-produced world of the early twentieth century. Modernist chairs—Le Corbusier's "machines for sitting"—were based on a standardized, male body. They proscribed a particular posture with no concessions to an individual's size, shape, or requirements. Modern industrial machines required humans to fit the machine, not vice versa.

In the first two decades after the Second World War, military research spurred new approaches to our relationship with machines, resulting in fields such as Human Factors Engineering. This evolved from two broad positions corresponding to human physical and cognitive abilities. That is, research into ergonomics on the one hand, and the psychological interaction between humans and machines on the other. Particularly in the United States, significant military research and investment in the 1940s and 1950s devised new methods of designing airplane cockpits, for example, and how humans might better operate radar and sonar technologies. Some of this research filtered out into other industries so that, for example, automotive designers learned from military cockpits to improve the design of automobile dashboards, pedals, and levers.

The other significant factor in the decades after the War was that the military, large corporations, and government increased their use of computers. Sold as processing machines, early computer systems occupied entire rooms and were rarely designed for ease of use by non-specialists. In a rare exception, in 1959, Ettore Stottsass designed Olivetti's Elea 9003 computer as a series of movable, modular cabinets. Stottsass's attention to human scale, ergonomics, and his symbolic use of color aimed to better integrate these machines into an office environment and reduce anxiety around using them. Under Thomas Watson Jr in the 1960s, IBM engaged various design consultants, including Eliot Noyes and George Nelson, to redesign the image of computing. Their standardized forms, reductive colors, and rational approach established the design language of IBM for decades afterwards: functional and efficient, but not exactly friendly.

Although integrated into offices, computers still required technical input languages and specialized training to operate, maintain, and repair. But, as computers spread to become a standard tool in various industries, non-specialist operators needed more intuitive means of communicating with these machines. During the 1960s and 1970s, researchers at Xerox Parc (Palo Alto Research Center) and MIT explored new ways of interacting with computers and new applications for them. Beyond simply calculating and processing data, with graphics and sound interfaces, researchers found that computers also had great potential as platforms for representation and communication.

Later known as "The Mother of All Demos," Doug Engelbart's oNLine System Demo at a 1968 San Francisco conference combined a number of innovations in a dramatic presentation. Collaborating with a remote lab via the first real-time video conference, Engelbart demonstrated the first computer mouse, using it to resize windows and highlight text on a screen. A breakthrough in interaction design, the mouse enabled computer users to manipulate virtual objects and move them around a screen. It also enabled users to interact with a computer via visual images rather than technical language. Although it took another decade for this technology to become truly user-friendly, reliable, and inexpensive, the mouse became an essential interactive tool.

The computer's input language, navigation, and storage systems remained issues for non-specialists. In 1982, the Xerox Star system proposed some novel solutions. The Star's "desktop" metaphor, developed by Tim Mott and Larry Tesler in Xerox Parc in the 1970s, comprised a screen arranged with virtual objects like on a physical desk. With the aid of a mouse, users could move files, documents, and printer icons around the screen, storing information in familiar ways. Over the next two decades, Apple and Microsoft adopted these ideas from the Star's interface. With the new Graphical User Interface (GUI) systems, users could manipulate objects on a screen rather than remembering and typing in complex command lines.

The 1984 Macintosh brought both the mouse and the GUI to a mass-consumer market. Compact and self-contained, the Mac was consciously designed to fit within the home. It appeared to be more like a kitchen appliance than a data processing machine. As we saw in Chapter 1, Susan Kare's graphics and icons, including the smiley-face Mac that appeared on the screen when it started up, created a usable and friendly interface. As well as the distinctive hardware, Apple's point-and-click interaction via the mouse replaced type input, making computing easier for home users. The spread of personal computing and a booming market for digital products resulted in the design of portable, lightweight computers in the form of laptops and hand-held PDAs (personal digital assistants).[1]

Popularized by designers such as Bill Moggridge and Bill Verplank, interaction design gradually came to be accepted as a new field of design. Originally trained as an industrial designer, Moggridge began to use the term after working on an early version of the laptop computer, the GRID Compass. Released in 1982, the GRID was used by NASA astronauts on space shuttle missions, and established many of the basic principles of later laptop designs. Moggridge realized that designing both the hardware and the software of new digital technologies with the end user in mind comprised a new discipline. Stemming from a mix of industrial and graphic designers, software and hardware engineers, psychologists, and anthropologists, interaction design consolidated over the 1990s and 2000s with conferences, associations, and specialized education.

In the late twentieth century, one of the problems that limited the use of new technologies was that interaction design was typically left to engineers or computer scientists. They developed machines that interested them and operated in ways they understood. But they had little empathy for or understanding of the needs of varied, non-specialist users. The introduction of user-centered or human-centered design methods into the development of digital technologies over the past two decades has changed this. Using interviews, observation, and anthropological methods, human-centered designers aim to increase an understanding of various users, their needs and desires in interacting with new technologies.

Affordances and scripts

Today, interaction design usually refers to digital products, systems, and services. But we also interact with more mundane, physical things, such as coffee mugs, washing machines, or automobiles. Such things enable us to perform everyday tasks, and their design can stimulate, provoke, or seduce us. But they can also frustrate or annoy us, making everyday tasks more difficult than they should be. For designers, how to design things that are intuitive, usable, and serve humans in an unobtrusive manner has long been a primary objective. To better understand our interaction with everyday things, some designers and critics characterize this relationship in terms of affordances or scripts. We will consider each in turn.

Assume for a moment that you have never seen a hammer. How would you know how to use it? Hammers do not come with an instruction manual. Instead, designers offer visual and tactile cues on their use. A colorful rubber grip, for example, clearly distinguishable from the silver steel head, proposes that this is where your hand should hold this object. Similarly, a child's bicycle handlebars are often designed with plastic hand grips with grooves that suggest where to place your fingers—the form invites you to grip the handlebars. In this way, cues about how we should interact with things are embedded in their physical forms.

We recognize and respond to colors, forms, textures, or materials more readily than reading instructions. The symbolic language of things discussed in Chapter 2 can also function as a guide to use, cues to aid operation, or constraints for safety. Designer and critic Donald Norman popularized the term "affordances" to describe how this works. "An affordance," he writes, "is a relationship between the properties of an object and the capabilities of the agent that determines just how the object could possibly be used. A chair affords ('is for') support and, therefore, affords sitting."[2] For Norman, a well-designed thing is one that uses visual or tactile cues to map its own operation so that users understand the relationship between the object's "operating controls" and its function.

That is, carefully designed products contain instructions for use without resorting to written manuals, notes, or labels. An electric toaster, for example, has a knob with numbers that corresponds to increasing or decreasing the heat of the internal elements, so users know that operating this knob makes the bread more or less toasted. In addition, machines provide us with "feedback" to confirm that our actions have occurred—clicks or beeps, for example—that let us know that the machine has responded, or a warning light to tell us to stop. As well as enable use, controls can also limit use, so that the toaster's heat control cannot go beyond a safe limit. Thinking through all the possible interactions and feedback between humans and machines in this way is a complex design challenge.

Consider another everyday example. Epinephrine autoinjectors, commonly known by the brand name EpiPen, are seemingly simple devices used to treat anaphylaxis for people with severe allergic reactions. A cylindrical form that looks like an oversized pen contains a fixed dose of epinephrine (adrenaline) and a hidden spring-loaded needle. When the user pushes one end, the needle exits the tip of the device and penetrates the patient's skin, delivering the drug into the patient. The original design, first approved by the U.S. Food and Drug Administration in 1987, featured tiny, complex text instructions that looked daunting in an emergency. Additionally, the pointy (needle) end was not obvious, which led to some mistakes in their operation.

Part of the problem lay in the pen metaphor. Whereas a pen has a cap over the pen tip, the EpiPen's cap was not over the needle tip, but on the opposite end. In a high-anxiety situation, some users, even trained healthcare professionals, unintentionally injected the adrenaline into their thumbs rather than into the patient. Despite these design issues, Mylan, the company that bought the patent for the EpiPen in 2007, dominated the market for drug delivery devices and had little incentive to change the design. In 2009, they altered the EpiPen's design with better attention to the affordances, including simplified text, visual instructions, and a label stating clearly which end the needle was.

But a 2017 Food and Drug Administration report documented hundreds of complaints of EpiPen activation failures and cases in which users had dispensed the drug incorrectly, some resulting in deaths.[3] This followed 2016 Congress hearings that Mylan was using their monopoly position to raise prices (in 2016, a two-pack rose to $600—for a drug that costs $1 in a device that costs perhaps $10 to make). Because of both the problematic design and price gouging, some emergency services personnel and general users have abandoned the EpiPen and returned to syringes or alternative "hacks" such as home-made drug-dispensing devices. Designing an effective drug-dispensing device is a greater challenge than initially imagined by the original designers. Yet trying to predict how people will interact with an apparently simple thing is fundamental for interaction designers.

A related way of understanding how interactions work is "scripting," in which products are understood as physically inscribed with a designer's or manufacturer's instructions for use. By way of explanation, philosopher Bruno Latour considers an example from traffic management. A city authority wants to make roads safer by slowing traffic. One option is to employ a traffic management person to stand by the road and tell each driver to slow down (expensive and impractical to scale up). Another is to install a road sign that says "slow down." This may encourage drivers to change their speed, but (if no one is watching) some drivers simply ignore it. Finally, a physical impediment such as a speed bump forces drivers to act (or risk damage to their vehicle). In this final option, a script ("slow down") is embedded into the design of our physical world—the speed bump alters driver behaviors.[4]

Human behavior is prescribed by designed constraints like this in many ways. Airport seating contains armrests to stop weary travelers from sleeping across seats. Authorities install "homeless spikes" on the ledges around a downtown office building, designed to keep homeless people from sleeping there. In various ways, nonhuman things play active roles in the drama of our lives. For Latour, these things are like characters that interact with humans according to certain predetermined scripts. In this way, designed things are often developed within particular scenarios and assumptions about users and their interactive behaviors. Like a script from a play or film, a designed product can prescribe its users how to act when they use it.

Rather than passive and neutral, Latour suggests that things have a certain agency, and this attribute can be—to some extent—determined by design. A takeaway, paper coffee cup, for example, contains the script, "throw me away after use." A ceramic cup's script contains the script, "wash me and use me again." Of course, there is nothing to stop people altering these scripts—reusing the paper cup or throwing away the ceramic cup—instead, they are a predicted sequence of actions. But, when used again and again, such scripts become embedded as cultural conventions and shape expectations we have about our interaction with things. From this perspective, designed objects invite certain actions and discourage others.

But the instructions embedded within a product are only ever based on an assumed sequence of actions and designing with scripts and affordances in mind involves predicting typical patterns and behaviors. Of course, humans are not always predictable and unintended actions are bound to occur. Users deviate from the script or find alternative affordances for designed things all the time. In fact, connections between a product's appearance and its possible uses might trigger an unintended action. A chair gives an affordance of sitting, for example, yet people also use chairs for standing on to reach a high cupboard, storing clothes on, hanging a towel over, or holding back a door on a windy day. As we saw in the last chapter with hacking, humans do not always follow a designer's carefully considered intentions.

A final crucial issue in designing for interaction follows from these considerations. Despite the language of scripts and things with agency, interaction between humans and things is not a conversation, nor is it the same as a relationship between two humans. A conversation between humans is a two-way exchange based on mutual intelligibility whereas things can only ever map a predetermined set of actions and interpretations. They do not adjust to a particular individual's needs, they cannot suggest an alternative if they sense our frustration or hear our exasperation.[5] That is, if the user veers off the intended script, the thing or machine cannot respond. Frustrated users of ATMs and self-checkout machines understand this limitation all too well.

CASE STUDY 5: THE DOOR

Architect Juhani Pallasmaa referred to a door handle as "the handshake of a building."[6] He intended this poetic description to inspire architects to design even the smallest details with careful regard to human interaction. But, like handshakes, doors and their handles can sometimes produce hesitation, frustration, or confusion. Do I pull or push? Push or slide? Do I wait for it to open automatically?

Donald Norman notes that interacting with a simple device such as a door should be straightforward. Ideally, he argues, "not only will the proper hardware operate the door smoothly, but it will also indicate just how the door is to be operated: it will incorporate clear and unambiguous clues."[7] Unfortunately, he notes that not all doors have such cues, or their cues are ambiguous or misleading. Some doors fail to indicate to users whether to push or pull, while others slide open but have a pull handle. Some doors require a sign to operate (chairs, after all, do not require a sign that says "sit").

In corporate offices, pull handles on both sides of a glass door are common (Figure 8), presumably because the symmetry makes the doors look balanced. Yet for users, from one side, the doors need to be pushed, from the other they need to be pulled, and there is no visual cue as to which is which. Vertical handles perfectly designed for grabbing with your hand and *pulling* toward you are misleading because you must *push* these doors to open them, leading to the

FIGURE 8 *Signs indicate how to use the doors of a New York office building.* Getty Images/Corbis Historical/James Leynse.

inclusion of written instructions. The seemingly simplest things are sometimes poorly designed from this perspective—light switches, water taps, office furniture—hence Norman's promotion of human-centered design.

Philosopher Bruno Latour has another perspective on doors. The invention of walls, he proposes, required openings to get in and out. Doors seemed a perfect invention until people forgot to close them. Human door closers and openers—doormen or grooms—were expensive, but automation could delegate the job of opening and closing to nonhuman things. A hinge and spring mechanism seemed the ideal solution.

But, while easier to control and discipline than humans, such nonhuman solutions have their own set of constraints. If made from heavy materials, for example, a door swings shut too fast. If it is too light, it may not close properly. People on crutches, in wheelchairs or children may find it difficult to enter or exit if the door's hinge and spring mechanism is not well-designed.

If, returning to Pallasmaa, a door handle is a handshake, should it be firm or relaxed? Or, in the case of automatic doors, dispensed with altogether? Even automatic doors that operate on the premise of sensing a user approaching and opening might be rescripted for more subtle interactions, suggest Wendy Ju and Larry Leifer. A designer might learn from a doorman, they argue, the automatic door "opening a little when a person walks by ... softly humming in overt preparation or jiggling its handle as enticement."[8]

Interface

After the digital revolution of the 1970s, the interaction between high-tech products, systems, and users emerged as an important aspect of design. Specialized fields such as HCI, interface design, and user experience (UX) design evolved in response to the perceived shortcomings of an engineering perspective in which new technologies were not developed or designed with the end user in mind, or were designed with only engineers in mind. These new fields developed interdisciplinary approaches to designing new technologies, typically drawing upon information and product design, as well as psychology, anthropology, linguistics, cognitive science, and computer science.

With the spread of digital devices, designers devoted increasing attention not only to the connections between humans and our machines, but also to how we interact with the virtual world. "Interface" is a term that refers to the boundary between the two, the almost invisible membrane that allows us to cross into another world and back again. Interface refers to both material and conceptual devices that enable (or disable) us in our interactions with digital technologies and with each other via those technologies. The screens, buttons, and digital hardware, as well as the software within, comprise a series of interfaces that mediate our relationship with the virtual realm. And they also mediate our experiences of space and social communication.

The spread of the touch screen with iPhones and iPads, for example, enabled a new type of interaction. To access the virtual world, users no longer needed a range of physical buttons to press, nor a keyboard or mouse. Instead, users could tap, swipe, drag, and pinch directly onto the screen. Earlier cellphones and computers, despite getting more compact, still used buttons for input and text-based menus. Although higher-resolution icons gradually replaced text, the interaction was still graphic and menu-driven. The new touch screens proved seductive in their almost invisible, almost seamless interaction between our fingers and the machine.

Touch screens merged the display and control elements of the interface so that a user's fingers become pointing devices. Direct manipulation, without menus, cursors, or physical pointing devices, changed the nature of the interaction, and allowed users to feel more in control. The mouse's double click was replaced by a tap, a flick to scroll through menu or options, a drag to change position of an icon, and pinching in or out to zoom. Such interactions have begun to alter user expectations of screens and response from machines.

As well as touch screens, recent innovations in gesture-based interactions enabled by spatial tracking offer further possibilities for human interaction with machines. Popularized through gaming systems, such as Nintendo's Wii-U and Microsoft's Kinect, users' body motions are an alternative means of interacting with machines. Although presently limited in their uses, gesture-based systems may have numerous future applications, rendering keyboards and mice obsolete. Augmented and virtual reality systems are still developing, with various goggles, gloves, and suits offering potential alternative means for us to interact with machines.

Importantly, we tend to think of interfaces as visual, no doubt due to our screen-dominated culture. But voice and touch-activated technologies are also offering new ways of interacting with machines. On one level, GPS navigation systems in automobiles speak directions, enabling drivers to concentrate on watching the road rather than looking at a screen. But, in more complex applications, for blind people, voice-controlled devices and apps for the home have been life-changing. The increasing use of smooth touch screens and visual displays are inaccessible to people with poor vision, and voice activated home appliances and devices enable a range of everyday activities, while for people with hearing impairments, touch sensitive, and vibrating devices offer alternative means of interaction.

In the mass-consumer marketplace, voice speaker assistants promise a further range of potential interactions. The earliest popular versions of the 2010s such as Apple's Siri, Microsoft's Cortana, and Amazon's Alexa, enable users to issue voice commands to operate household devices, play music, search for information such as news or weather forecasts, or connect to lighting and heating systems. Combining voice synthesizers with voice recognition technology, these small, speaker-like devices decode human speech and reply with appropriate responses. Yet the first generation of these devices highlights some particular problems in how to design interactions with "smart" things.

The fact that they are all female voices is not coincidental. After all, we assume our robots to be recognizably of a lower status, so such devices reproduce gender stereotypes about power and subservience. Projecting both warmth and compliance, the feminine voices are also programmed with particular verbal patterns that let users know who's in charge—they apologize when they do not understand and use excessive personal pronouns to reinforce their submissive status.[9] But even as this relationship is played out, exactly how these devices are monitoring, tracking, and compiling data about us is also a concern. Whether we are creating pliable servants or surveillance devices is part of an ongoing debate surrounding the design of such interactive systems.

Designer and researcher Brenda Laurel usefully characterized the interactive relationship we have with new technologies as a form of theater in which humans and computers create an ongoing dramatic performance.[10] Computer games—from Super Mario Brothers to Fortnite—have long been at the forefront in expanding how we perform actions in imaginary worlds. Via a combination of user input and visual, auditory, and other sensory responses from the computer, we engage in a sensory experience akin to an immersive, theatrical performance. And lessons from successful video games have been transferred into other types of apps, combining entertainment with informative content, such as for museums, for example.

This concept, Laurel argues, works equally well for more "serious" computing too. As in a computer game, at work we are similarly immersed in a document or spreadsheet, cutting and pasting, searching and saving. Importantly, the "technical magic," or the interface comprising hardware, software programs and applications, provides a stage for these dynamic interactions. As an alternative way of understanding our interaction with computers, Laurel's theater gives agency to various designed components such that our performances are ongoing collaborations that are both scripted, yet ideally allow room for improvisation too.

Software

Beyond the material components of interaction design, designing software is another critical and growing field. From an initial engineering, problem-solving approach to a more recent human-centered approach, designing software has evolved to incorporate a better understanding of user needs and expectations. Understood as another type of interface between humans and machines, software is a "kind of translator, mediating between the two parties, making one sensible to the other."[11] The complexity of designing software interfaces is often underestimated, and the multitude of seemingly small decisions adds up to a better or a worse final interface.

Consider the design of a relatively simple website. Designers need to decide whether to use buttons, text boxes, or drop-down menus for input; sliders, tags, or icons for navigation; notification or message boxes for feedback. How to display a website's content as well as the best ways for users to interact with that content involves a series of design decisions. How to ensure the website is clear and easy to use yet with enough options and choices for the user? Graphic design and typography also remain a crucial element ensuring legibility, consistency, and establishing a consistent personality or brand. Adding another layer of complexity, websites are typically not a single page but part of a larger system, in which case all these elements need to be scalable, ideally modular components that work across various pages, ensuring consistency and predictability.

Beyond the visual, designers have extended the GUI interfaces of the 1980s and 1990s—icons, folders, and menus—to include other types of user interactions such as sound, touch, and gestures. Smartphones and gaming consoles have moved beyond the early paradigms of interaction based on static GUI interfaces. But even on stand-alone computers, the desktop metaphor is also changing as interface design shifts to mobile devices and touch screens, and new graphic applications allow for animation and moving components. Part of the challenge for interface designers working with software is designing coherent structures that are compatible across various platforms.

As we saw in Chapter 1, we could begin designing software from basic building blocks, such as words or icons, but designing interfaces in the form of programs or apps or websites entails an additional set of limitations driven by what the computer and programmers can do. There is also the issue of user expectations and limitations. Users who have grown accustomed to navigating Microsoft Word, for example, with its multiple drop-down menus, task bars with buttons, and a scroll bar along the left hand side, come to expect similar menus and bars in other software programs. Although this may not be the best way of designing software, it becomes a conventional language, a recognizable structure and way of interaction that users become accustomed to.

In the world of complex menus, navigation systems and options that developed over the 1980s and 1990s, no wonder the simplicity of Google's search engine page proved popular when it went live in 1999. Free of clutter and images (apart from the logo), the interface was strikingly simple: a single input bar with two choices—"Google Search" or "I'm Feeling Lucky." Of course, the search algorithm behind the scenes was not simple, but for users, the simplicity and clarity of the interface and speed of the search made Google extremely popular. But the simplicity and user friendliness soon concealed an infrastructure devoted not only to searching for information—however that is defined by Google's page ranking algorithm—but also to maximizing advertising revenue.

As Google discovered, in interface design, response time is crucial. By pressing a key or mouse button or swiping a screen, users expect an instant result. But, even with processing speeds increasing, some things still take time. Hence the design of progress indicators to reassure users. Little dialog boxes with a bar, for example, indicate the status of a process and communicate feedback from the machine to the user. Users also need feedback to know when they have made a mistake. Rather than early interface responses such as "Syntax Error," newer software responds with language such as "Oops, something's gone wrong." In this way, programmers have designed a more user-friendly response into the interface. Such "natural language" interactions are becoming more widespread.

From a user's perspective, navigating an interface should ideally be structured along clear paths. These may be links and options in the form of text, buttons, or images, but they should be consistent and familiar to users.

Initially based in graphical forms, designers now have the option of creating navigation systems with animation, video, or sound. While on the one hand, interface designers strive for universal usability for people with various abilities and skills, on the other, they also strive to stand out in a crowded digital world. Engaging visuals, storytelling, or motion graphics can work to capture and maintain a user's attention or elicit an emotional response.

A balance between simplicity and universality and engagement is displayed by websites such as that of Airbnb. The site's home page includes simple yet compelling photographs and inviting text ("unique homes and experiences") that elicit an emotional reaction from users. The landing page begins with a textbox, "Where do you want to go?," then proceeds to particular dates and details, encouraging users to explore further after the initial, simple question. The site offers clear subsequent steps to input data (where, when, and other accommodation options), and images of exotic destinations and experiences to encourage exploration. The navigation then combines a map with possible houses for rent and additional information such as descriptions, star ratings, and prices.

Using a similar aesthetic but different means of interaction, crowdfunding websites aim to engage and provoke action in users to pledge money. Kickstarter, for example, features simple graphics and text, a short video explainer of each project and recommendations reinforced by social proof—that is, how many people have already pledged. Users are further encouraged by text noting the limited time and limited bonuses. Color contrast highlights the prominent pledge button, which then offers levels of commitment via set amounts of money to pledge. Importantly, such sites typically emphasize a sense of purpose, social good, or sense of community, and include interactive triggers that send potential pledgers reminders to follow-up, encouraging later interaction.

Another key issue in digital interaction is user control. Or, at least making users feel like they have some control over processes and interactions rather than the complete automation of tasks. But in some instances, automation can make things easier for users. Auto-fill input boxes, for example, that repeat data you have already typed can reduce a mundane task for users. Flexibility is also crucial. In other ways, interfaces have built-in capabilities for users to change preferences, set parameters such as color schemes, sizes, or menu arrangement. Importantly, such flexibility in software design allows the interface to meet different needs or users with different abilities.

For a major brand like Google, interface design is crucial, particularly as it has grown beyond just a search engine. From its beginnings, Google was focused on an engineer's ideal of efficiency—speed was the metric that mattered most, and visuals simply slowed down user interactions with the search engine. This approach made sense in the early 2000s, particularly before broadband internet access became widespread. As we saw above, for the search engine website, a simple design proved successful. But, with the addition of more programs and software either acquired from other companies or designed by them, Google's varied software offerings were no longer consistent.

Launched in 2014, Google's Material Design language for phones, tablets, and desktop computers aimed to create a coherent, unified language across their software and across various platforms and scales. This included consistency of user interactions, so that Google designers unified the menus and colors across their products such as Gmail, Google Docs, Google Maps, and YouTube. Three parallel lines in a circle icon, for example, now stands for "main menu" across all Google products, menus open on the left hand side, and Arial is the default font (as it is widely supported and readable). Such an effort in redesigning their digital interface helped not only in standardizing experiences for users but also in reinforcing a coherent brand for the company.

CASE STUDY 6: THE IPHONE

At the 2007 iPhone launch, Apple CEO Steve Jobs, in his signature black turtleneck and blue jeans, proclaimed, "An iPod, a phone, and an internet communicator. An iPod, a phone ... Are you getting it? These are not three separate devices, this is *one device*." The iPhone shifted the popular concept of the phone as a communication device to the phone as a device with which we consume music, videos, games, produce photos, animations and films, a navigation device, an alarm clock, and a calendar (Figure 9). Not quite instantaneously, but over the next decade, two billion people around the world integrated smartphones into their lives.

In the 1980s, the first popular mobile phones were adaptations of telephones, while the second generation in the 1990s were lighter, pocket-sized and included features such as text messaging, games, and cameras. The design of the iPhone drew from these conventions as well as its own internal design logic, developed in earlier Apple products such as the iMac and the iPod. Apple's attention to design, led by Jobs and later Jonathan Ive, head of the Industrial Design Group, included not only products but also packaging, advertising, and graphics.

Apple's product design language drew upon that of Dieter Rams, head designer at Braun through the 1960s and 1970s. His thoughtful, clear, and concise electronic products such as a calculator, radio, and electric shaver inspired both Jobs and Ive. Jobs's legendary attention to detail—the curve of the edge, the menu bar, the logo, the lines—resulted in a design-led company whose aesthetic consistency, efficiency of materials, and reduction of complexity set the bar for digital devices.

FIGURE 9 *The first generation iPhone, 2007. Getty Images/Axel Schmidt.*

The iPhone introduced three significant innovations. First was the touch screen. Swiping, pinching, pushing, and tapping the screen was a novel means of interacting with a digital device and made the screen (rather than physical buttons) the central focus. Second was the software, particularly the inclusion of apps, extensions that could transform a phone into a navigation device, a dating service, or a flashlight. The third was its seamless connection to the internet, which, combined with apps, enabled a whole new range of possibilities.[12]

Initially, Apple tried to maintain a closed system that limited third-party app development but quickly, as a platform for apps, the iPhone slipped from Apple's control. In less than a year, the iPhone spawned similar Android smartphones from Google, Samsung, and others, which imitated the key innovations and added their own. Although mass produced, smartphones offered numerous personalization features—from personal ringtones, screensaver, or crocheted cases bought from Etsy to sophisticated app modifications and hacks.

Smartphones also brought about broader social and cultural changes, reconfiguring notions of private and public space, and initiating a culture of "always on." They initiated new types of social communication—both on an individual level (in the form of continual updates, images, and interactions) and on a mass level with social media platforms—and thus inaugurated cultural changes.

In 2010, employee suicides at Shenzhen factories drew attention to the plight of hundreds of thousands of Chinese laborers who create Apple products (and Nintendo, Sony, and Microsoft products). Low wages, unpaid overtime, and monotonous assembly-line work highlighted what "designed in California, assembled in China" actually meant. Even a mass-produced smartphone required hand crafting, from fastening chip boards to packaging, a complex hidden labor process.

And, despite its reductive use of materials and efficient packaging, Apple is not a company renowned for sustainable design. Even after a scathing Greenpeace report in 2007, Apple was relatively slow to improve energy efficiency and battery life of their devices. Ultimately, iPhones—like all smartphones—use toxic rare earth materials, are not designed to be repaired or recycled, and their constant model upgrades continue the idea of planned obsolescence into the twenty-first century.

Smart things

Despite the contemporary hype around smart things, connecting material things to a network or embedding technological devices into everyday life is not new. From the 1970s, for example, RFID (radio frequency identification) tags have been attached to products for tracking and inventory, electronic toll collection, and security purposes. But in the twenty-first century, as digital technologies shrunk, and processing power and information storage capacity came down in price, the idea of ubiquitous computing or the Internet of Things started to become a possibility. Potentially, digital devices built into furniture, clothes, houses, and streets might create the seamless integration of a myriad physical things to a networked, virtual world. While this is some way off, various "smart" things are now everyday products, such as the smartphone (Case Study 6).

INTERACTION

The idea of adding digital interfaces and connectivity to existing everyday products has been around for a while, and with it, promises of life-changing transformations. We tend to forget the failures. Computers designed to be integrated into the kitchen, for example, have been through many unsuccessful iterations. Launched in 2000, the Audrey was one of the first computers designed specifically for the kitchen. Its small screen, curved housing, and knob control like an old-fashioned TV offered internet connectivity but little else. The Icebox, launched in 2001, functioned as a hub to connect various smart kitchen appliances such as a microwave and coffeemaker. Both failed to appeal to users, as did numerous prototypes of internet refrigerators during the early 2000s (the first to make it to stores, LG's Digital Multimedia Fridge of 2003, quickly disappeared).

Perhaps the problem was that such devices lacked a clear function. Does connecting a fridge to the internet make a better fridge? Do people really need a kitchen computer when they already have one in the lounge room? The unification of fridge and computer added nothing useful to existing fridges. Combined with the facts that the speed of computer technology moves faster than fridges (which people use for a decade or more), and the retail price of the two devices together proved prohibitively expensive, it was no wonder kitchen computers failed to take off. Ultimately, it seems there was little justification for designing a fridge embedded with a computer, although new touch screen and voice activation controls by several manufacturers suggest new versions of the smart fridge are still being designed.[13]

More successful, wearable devices offer more useful interactions between humans and machines. In the 2010s, the fad for wearable fitness devices such as the Fitbit and Jawbone introduced new possibilities. These comprised a flexible plastic bracelet embedded with a chip that tracks activity such as steps walked and heart rate and delivers them via an app in the form of personalized metrics. Launched in 2009, the Fitbit soon spawned similar devices and variations that could monitor and aggregate personal data about physical activities or health-related information. While primarily aimed at a consumer market for tracking personal fitness, the numerous medical uses for such wearable "personal informatic tools" are still being explored, and the ability to collate and represent an even broader range of personal data may have a wide range of future applications.

The miniaturization of digital components means that interfaces are changing to become almost invisible and increasingly ubiquitous in our physical environment. Often referred to as the "Internet of Things," the idea of embedded interfaces within everyday objects suggests the prospect of connecting all manner of things to the internet and to each other. Tags and sensors along roads and sidewalks, for example, can draw data from passing traffic and pedestrians to enable better city planning. In some such future scenarios, the interface disappears from sight, and we may not know when we are interacting with the virtual world. Issues around privacy and surveillance, as well as changes in how we relate to space and, possibly, to each other, may generate the significant design challenges of the near future.

Although in its infancy, the concept of the Internet of Things tends to be centered on developing smart things rather than thinking about things in relation to people. That is, the interactive component often comes last in developing such technologies. There is a risk in humans becoming passive recipients of smart things or integrated into a smart network of things that they cannot interact with or do not adequately understand. That is, design questions such as what is it that these smart things are going to help people achieve or how they will make their lives better? In the rush to design ever smarter devices, designers risk losing sight of how these things might afford independence, maintain social relations, foster creativity, or help their various users.

Robots

Robotics is still relatively new, yet some simple robots have already made their way into people's lives and designing HRIs promises to be a growing design field. In 2002, iRobot, a robotics company founded in 1990, launched the first version of their simple, consumer robot, the Roomba Discovery vacuum cleaner. This small, circular device navigates around a home to clean floors. Using rotating brushes to sweep the floor and a vacuum to suck up dust and particles, the Roomba is embedded with infrared sensors. These sensors avoid walls and furniture, and detect and adapt to changes in level. Later versions of the robot with an internet-connected app allow users to schedule cleaning times and access status reports remotely.

As the first such vacuum robot, the iRobot inspired other companies to produce versions with similar forms and functions. Their intention was to replace monotonous housework with autonomous machines. Yet more than this, research suggests that users interact with robots such as the Roomba in a human-like way, by giving it a name, ascribing it a personality and helping it dust in those hard-to-get-places. And, as we saw with IKEA in the last chapter, Roomba has also proven a good machine for hackers to experiment with. In fact, the Roomba comes with a serial port that allows hackers to modify the robot by connecting it to a computer and modifying the programming. In this way, the Roomba has been modified to play games, draw pictures, and star in YouTube cat videos.

At this stage, a humanoid robot remains in the realm of science fiction. The design of robots is varied and it remains to be seen whether humanoid robots are designable or desirable. Robots such as the voice-activated assistants such as Alexa or the vacuuming Roomba blend in with other household appliances and perform a limited number of specific tasks. But designing human-like robots remains a goal of some researchers. Technological achievement dominates this field, yet there is much for designers to consider in helping to develop useful robots. No doubt affected by images of R2-DT, C-3PO, or a host of other cinematic robots, for many people, robot design can evoke pleasure or fear.

The initial interactions between humans and robots occur through our perception of form, color, materials, size, and sounds. Patterns of movement and functions also affect how we interact with robots. At present, the most promising contemporary design for robot applications are in assistive care, particularly in Japan, where experiments and prototypes of assistive robots are at the forefront. Researchers working with robots hope their designs might help the elderly at home with physical tasks or remind them of events. In these situations, balancing standardized design with robots that can adapt to individual users' contexts and daily schedules is an ongoing challenge.

Through their conceptual or "Critical Design" projects, designers Anthony Dunne and Fiona Raby present a critical perspective of our interactions with new technology. Their "Technological Dreams Series: No.1, Robots," for example, comprised a series of four imaginary domestic robots and a video featuring a perplexed woman who is not sure how to interact with them. Number 3 robot, for example, looks like a twisted wooden table top with two eyes at one end—it is, the designers write, "a sentinel, it uses retinal scanning technology to decide who accesses our data ... This robot demands that you stare into its eyes for a long time, it needs to be sure it is you."[14] They raise issues of privacy, data access, and biometric access—but also present an oddly intimate interaction—a quirky, critical response to futuristic technologies.

Alongside the utopian visions of a technological future driven by servile robots and smart things, there is also the dystopian vision of a world of interconnected devices running out of our control. Controlled by large corporations, governments, or individuals, such technologies might also track our every move, purchase, heartbeat, and personal connection in a kind of prison enabled by ubiquitous computing. Some critics have raised the ideas of increased surveillance, coercion, and paranoia that may result from the widespread dissemination of smart technologies. In terms of interaction, humans may find themselves enmeshed in technological systems that shape how we act and think, increasingly losing any understanding of how they all work. But for now, robots are designed as discrete combinations of hardware and software incompatible with other robots.

A final series of issues arise from unrecognized or hidden assumptions of interaction design. The first is that technology-focused and engineering professionals are traditionally male domains so inevitably there is a male bias in the design of technological products, hardware, and software. Despite the overarching ideal of technological progress as inherently neutral, it is not. Not only have male designers dominated the digital high-tech industries but also they have shown little interest in women as users—their needs, values, interests, or priorities rarely enter into the design and development of high-tech products. Automated systems are also increasingly under scrutiny over opaque algorithms designed with systematic bias that codify various types of discrimination.[15]

Attention to particular users is worth considering further. In interaction design, the ideal user is typically genderless, yet design is contextual and the gender of real users directly affect interactions. Sexual harassment in social media and virtual worlds, for example, is a common phenomenon—and design based on gender assumptions shapes our interactions online in profound ways.[16] The ideal user also typically resides in the United States and many of the technologies discussed above are designed from this perspective. Interaction designers are slowly coming round to the idea that one apparently timeless, universal user does not account for the multitude of cultural, social, and regional differences in user experience. As we saw in previous chapters, a singular design to fit everyone is problematic—interaction practices, like people, rarely conform to universal standards.

Recognizing interaction as central to design has meant designers ideally aim to create flexible or fluid scenarios or strategies that acknowledge active user participation. Further results of this acknowledgment of the user include the emerging specialization in more holistic "experience design" that integrates new technologies, systems, and services, as well as the dissolution of a mass market in favor of ever-more singular experiences (discussed further in Chapter 5). Design, conceived like this, requires an ethical foundation. Imagining end users as "ethical agents" rather than simply users or consumers and the design process framed as a "relation of reciprocity" seem valuable first steps. But, with the increasing complexity of design practices and processes, and the larger interdisciplinary teams required to achieve complex designed artifacts, systems, and services, the issue of responsibility remains a difficult ethical one.

Finally, the projected increase in interactive devices, surfaces, and things raises a number of concerns for interaction design. At what point do we risk becoming overwhelmed or confused by the profusion of constant interactivity? Already, parents fear their children are becoming addicted to video games while they themselves may be equally addicted to interaction with their smartphones. The seductive demands and feedback of both are designed to keep us continually engaged. A sense of a loss of control might result in banning video games or switching off social media, yet these are only ever temporary. Understanding and managing interactivity may be a crucial life skill of the next generation and for designers, less interaction may prove to be just as valuable as better interaction.

Chapter summary

- Design for interactions considers how humans use and experience things
- Designed things can proscribe their users' actions and behaviors
- Interfaces serve as a connection between users and machines
- Hardware and software design enables our interaction with computers and each other
- Smart, networked things, and robots present significant future design challenges

4

Systems and Services

Things are embedded in systems of production, distribution, and consumption. These systems, as well as the interactions we have with numerous services every day, are an increasingly essential component of contemporary design. While things are tangible, systems and services are intangible processes, connections, and interactions. Design practice in government or financial consultancies, for example, often produces minimal physical outcomes, yet aids people in achieving their goals. An increased attention to systems and services by designers is directly related to the spectacular growth of the service sector over the past two or three decades. In the United States in 2016, for example, less than 7 percent of the population was employed in manufacturing things, while 80 percent of the population was employed in services.[1] As manufacturing shifted offshore, service provisions increased, particularly in health, leisure, and hospitality, and designers have responded.

The changing way we listen to music and watch movies is illustrative of these changes. In the late twentieth century, in order to listen to their favorite song, people bought a vinyl record or cassette tape to play on a stereo system. In the late 1980s and 1990s, the digital compact disc supplanted records and tapes. In the early 2000s, online distribution enabled people to buy music in an intangible, digital format from an online store such as iTunes, and then enabled subscription services such as Spotify. Over the same time period, the shift from video cassettes to DVDs to online distribution services such as Netflix followed the same pattern. Now, to listen to music or watch movies, we no longer need to buy a physical product, but instead subscribe to a service. This shift—from products to a mix of products, systems, and services—continues to have profound implications for designers.

Systems

In 1954, when milkshake mixer salesman Ray Kroc visited Maurice and Richard McDonald's hamburger stand in San Bernardino, California, he was impressed by the assembly line production, self-service system, and simple menu. In his subsequent contract with the brothers, Kroc replicated their system, menu, and store design, building over 1,000 McDonald's restaurants around the United States over the next decade. The end products—hamburgers, fries, and milkshakes—were not innovative, yet the system and service provision were incredibly successful. Refined and extended over the next half century, Kroc's system proved robust enough to repeat in over 30,000 restaurants all around the world.

For customers, McDonald's products are relatively standard in quality and variety across stores, as is the self-service system in which they serve themselves and dispose of their own waste. Behind the scenes, precise and standardized food production and workflow systems ensure consistency and uniformity. A combination of interchangeable, low-wage workers and machines are ordered into a smooth workflow process. The design of such systems is calculated to be as efficient as possible to ensure predictable outcomes at the fastest possible speed, delivered at the lowest possible cost.

This systematic approach to delivering products, termed "McDonaldization" by sociologist George Ritzer, is characterized by "efficiency, calculability, predictability and control."[2] Of course, its commercial success not only influenced McDonald's fast food competitors, but aspects were adopted in other industries. Zara and H&M's fast fashion model, for example, is similarly based on efficient production, distribution, and consumption systems. IKEA's global success is similarly attributable to its emphasis on self-service, standardization, and efficient systems (see Case Study 7).

Modular systems, comprising interchangeable components that can be assembled in various ways, are another means by which designers create systems. A well-known and much-loved example is Lego. In the 1950s, the Danish toy-making company began experimenting with plastic bricks, eventually patenting a "stud and tube" system that allowed standardized geometric bricks to interlock in various combinations. With only a little variation in standard brick forms, users can build an incredible variety of structures. Modular systems have also proved popular in office furniture (notably Herman Miller and Steelcase), in home furnishings (notably IKEA furniture), and in computing hardware and software design. In such cases, standardized components lower manufacturing costs, but flexible configurations allow consumers to adapt the systems to their specific needs.

We have already encountered wayfinding systems (in Chapter 1) and coherent product lines (in Chapter 2) but in considering systems, it is important to understand the relationship and interactions between various components. From a design perspective, a system, as a set of interconnected things coherently related or organized, should be designed to achieve some ultimate purpose or function.[3] As a collective unity, a system includes interdependent elements, as in a transport system composed of trains and buses, tracks and roads, timetables, and drivers. A systems approach encourages designers to think in combinations of tangible and intangible elements, physical and digital components, as well as human and nonhuman agents. Ultimately, this involves analyzing the interactions of a system's components in context rather than each component in isolation.

Apple's iPod, for example, was not just an innovative new device, but enabled users to access a music delivery system. Previous mobile music players, such as the Sony Walkman, required users to buy and carry around multiple cassettes for storing music. But, with the launch of iTunes in 2003 and increased internet accessibility, Apple's iPod became not just a lightweight music player with a simple interface, but a seamless music distribution and management system. The "product" was the device, its interface, and iTunes, a digital music platform that promised "a thousand songs in your pocket" plus a means to organize and store them. Over the next decade, the iTunes store became the world's largest online music seller and the iPod's various iterations sold over 400 million units. Apple's innovative assemblages of product, systems, and services continued with the iPhone (see Case Study 6).

Designing such Product Service Systems (PSS), comprising a mix of tangible things and intangible systems and services, has inaugurated a shift for designers. Rather than designing singular things to fulfil a particular need, designers are increasingly focused on thinking about how this need may be achieved via different means. These include designing systems based on customer access to physical products rather than ownership, for example, or systems that provide access to libraries of digital music or video content as with Spotify or Netflix. A fundamental design question is asking what the "value-in-use" to customers is and, ultimately, what they actually need. Rethinking mobility in systems terms rather than car or bicycle ownership, for example, results in car-sharing or bicycle-sharing systems. Such systems inevitably require some kind of material devices and interfaces, making such an approach to design profoundly collaborative and cross-disciplinary.

In 2009, Amsterdam-based Rau Architects approached the lighting manufacturer Philips with a novel idea: what they really wanted was light in their offices, but without buying the bulbs, lamps, cabling, and other infrastructure associated with lighting. The architects worked with Philips to design an intelligent lighting system that responded to changes in daylight levels and the needs of their different workspaces. Philips then supplied the infrastructure and took responsibility for maintenance, reusing, and recycling it, while the architects paid an ongoing fee. The project's success led Philips to introduce a "pay per lux" system, whereby companies pay a regular fee for Philips to design, install, maintain, and upgrade their lighting systems, and then only pay for the light ("lux") they consume.

Amsterdam's Schiphol Airport adopted this system, and it may have broader application such as for public lighting in cities. Importantly, rather than selling physical light bulbs or lamps, Philips is selling lighting as a service, and it is in its interest to ensure that its systems are energy efficient, cheap to install, repairable, and recyclable. For Schiphol, for example, Philips designed modular lighting systems in which components are easy to repair, replace, and recycle (whereas most lighting components today are designed to be simply thrown away). Potentially, models such as these combine circular resource use with a convenient solution for companies or institutions. By creating a system of products, service, and supporting infrastructure, a PSS can address customer needs in a more energy and resource efficient, and ultimately, more sustainable way.

In the early years of Industrial Modernization, designers, manufacturers, and consumers tended to think in linear terms. That is, we extract raw materials from the earth with which we design, produce, and consume things, then discard them as waste. This is the "take-make-waste" model. By the late twentieth century, limited natural resources, industrial pollution, and the degradation of ecosystems led many to question this model. From the Whole Earth Catalogue and environmental movement to Buckminster Fuller's mathematically-driven analysis of the limited resources of "spaceship earth," the idea of the planet as an interconnected system took hold. For design, this initially meant an emphasis on thinking about recyclability, new ways of minimizing materials, design for repair and disassembly, or simply living with *less* material things.

But we still tend to envisage systems as closed. That is, to really begin thinking systematically, we need to consider how one system interacts with other systems. To return to the McDonald's example, while we understand the efficient product and service delivery system is designed to deliver affordable food to customers, the way it interacts with larger systems remains hidden. What are the economic effects of fast food production on agricultural systems or the environmental effects of fast food packaging waste? What are the social effects of a service system founded on low wages? Or, what are the effects on public health when a large portion of the population are consuming high-fat, high-sugar food? Replicated on a mass scale, the ripple effect of one system on a host of related systems can become a tidal wave.

An alternative model that we encountered in Chapter 3 is McDonough and Braungart's "cyclical, cradle-to-cradle biological system."[4] Modern industrial culture, they argue, is based on cradle to grave design in which we "take-make-waste." Some of the solutions they propose include using compostable bio-materials and transforming product-based solutions into services. They also argue that manufacturers, rather than consumers, should assume responsibility for recycling the materials used in industrial mass production, an idea already taken up into some degree in Germany. Recent European Union proposals to limit planned obsolescence by making physical products easier to repair and recycle are another notable innovation. Rethinking our designed systems often takes us into the realm of organizational and policy design, issues to which we will return to in Chapter 6.

CASE STUDY 7: IKEA

Founded in 1943 by seventeen-year-old Ingvar Kamprad as a mail-order service, IKEA evolved into a distributor of flat-packed furniture. In 1961, because of a Swedish furniture cartel which boycotted IKEA's low prices, IKEA began to source products from Poland (where costs were also 50 percent lower than in Sweden). The boycott also forced IKEA to design their own furniture and to adapt their designs to both available resources and the limitations of flat-packaging. From the beginning, IKEA's success lay in systems and services.

Certainly, IKEA's classic products, such as the POÄNG armchair, BILLY bookcase, and IVAR storage system, have survived for over thirty years. But, like McDonald's products, these things are not particularly innovative. What is innovative is the system that enables Russian pine, prepared in Poland, designed in Sweden, and shipped as a flat-pack to Australia, to be assembled by a customer into a useful piece of furniture. For IKEA's designers, such complex global systems represent a challenge to attain maximum efficiency from materials and packaging at the cheapest possible price.

Singular products also function within furniture ensembles and larger storage, kitchen or bathroom systems. The IKEA kitchen planner, for example, via 3D modeling software, allows customers to mix and match components such as cabinets, sink units, and electrical appliances to create complete kitchens. From their virtual kitchen design, customers can keep track of the cost of individual components and order them online. IKEA's kitchen system thus incorporates not only modular components, but also the associated software system linked to stock control and installation rates.

In stores, limited service encourages the customer to find products and use a self-checkout, which both increases customer involvement and ensures retail efficiency (Figure 10). Complex or large products are designed to be assembled by the customer at home, thus including interaction and participation by the end user into the system. But, while for some customers, completing the furniture provokes a certain satisfaction, for others, it provokes confusion or frustration.

FIGURE 10 *Self-serve shelves in IKEA, Miami, 2017. Getty Images/Jeffrey Greenberg/UIG.*

Regardless, IKEA's success has led other furniture manufacturers and retailers to adapt these systems.

Following a rigorous logic, IKEA's systematic approach to design encompasses typography and signage, individual products, spatial layout, software and logistics systems, and its organizational structure. This helps achieve a coherent corporate image and consistency across their website, catalogue, products, packaging, and stores. IKEA's "total design"—from the flag to the meatballs—works to color both the experience and the products with an image of Swedish-ness, regardless of each store's global location or the origin of the products.[5]

Mapping services

The rise of the service sector and possibilities enabled by new technologies have resulted in a rising interest in design for services. A relatively new field, service design aims to create better services for customers, and includes a bundle of skills and expertise drawn from communication design, product design, and interaction design, as well as marketing, anthropology, and other social sciences. One of the first issues designers have confronted in this realm is how to visualize or communicate a service. That is, if products are tangible things that exist in time and space, designing them via sketches, models, or prototypes is straightforward. But if services are invisible, how do we visualize them?

In the 1980s, G. Lynn Shostack, a banking executive who approached services from a marketing and management perspective, examined ways to document a design process that includes both tangible and intangible components. Because of the lack of documentation models, Shostack concluded, services tend to be designed via poorly articulated oral and written instructions. To alleviate this problem, she proposed "a system which will allow the structure of a service to be mapped in an objective and explicit manner ... a service blueprint."[6] A service blueprint was essentially a flowchart diagram that mapped a sequence of events, specifically the processes within a company and how each process interacts with customers and with other processes. A service blueprint proved a useful visual document to map the customer "journey" through a new service, and enabled designers to test and modify it before its eventual delivery to customers.

Another key service term is "touchpoints." Typically, these are points of interaction between consumers and the company. These need not be only physical, but can include a website, app, print marketing, as well as physical products or a store. That is, all encounters a customer has with the company, its products, and services. From a marketing perspective, customer touchpoints contribute to the company's "story" or brand narrative, so that ideally, designers aim to create a coherent, clear message across them all. Designing across a service system also includes thinking about a company's range of resources and infrastructure, including staff, products, physical environment, organizational structure, and administrative systems. Touchpoints, as the tangible evidence of services, are the physical aspect of what the designer designs, yet they are fundamentally interactive, as they require the engagement of customers to make the service complete.

A final key term worth elaborating is "servicescape," a term adopted from hospitality, retail, and tourism that describes the physical environment where services take place and the staff and customers are involved. This includes architectural and interior design—not only spatial layout—but the ambience created by décor, furnishings, lighting, music, smell, and physical comfort levels. These varied elements combine to affect a customer's experience of the service, and therefore should be carefully designed to create a particular impression. A store's signage, for example, can set the mood via typography or graphics, a machine pumps out enticing smells by the door, and lighting draws customers in. Beyond functional interactions, service design can also engage our senses.

In some contexts, designers draw upon a theatrical metaphor, dividing a service between front- and back-stage activities and roles played by both staff and customers. In a restaurant, for example, a closed kitchen may be designed for staff only, as it is a backstage area in which cooking and food preparation occur. But an open kitchen shifts cooks, wait staff, and cooking from behind the scenes to front-stage, which requires a different approach to designing the physical space and staff behaviors. Here, "the factory cannot be hidden and may in fact have a strong impact on customers' perceptions of the service experience."[7] Importantly, the design of the physical environment in which services occur is crucial not only in achieving end goals, but also in communicating values to consumers and encouraging motivation for employees.

Although such ideas about designing services were first developed in the 1980s and 1990s, service design as a specific profession only began in the early 2000s when the first specialist service design studios such as Engine and LiveWork established consultancies. As a distinct field, service design borrowed from existing design disciplines—particularly product, communication, interaction, and interior design—and from marketing and management. Originally focused on interfaces and interactions, service design's other distinction was coproduction and participatory design (which we will return to below). Whereas the designer's contribution to services had formerly been marginal or piecemeal—designing an interface, designing a new product, or designing a new space—service design as a discipline embraced a more holistic role.

Designer Lucy Kimbell argues that there are two primary developments that contributed to the growth of service design. First, networked media technologies have changed traditional design outputs; and second, management theory and practice have started paying attention to design's role in innovation, marketing, and change. In the latter, the designer's role has been identified as threefold: "through their insights into consumers and end-users, evidenced in their human-centered approach and methods; through their iterative processes of idea generation, modeling and prototyping, testing and selection, often involving multidisciplinary teams; and through their competences in working with aesthetics and visual forms."[8] According to Kimbell, as services are intangible and dynamic, and because of the intimate involvement of the consumer, services are heterogeneous and therefore require a different approach to designing mass-produced, standardized products.

One of the earliest service design consultancies, the UK-based Engine Design, completed several projects with Virgin airlines to enhance passenger services that illustrate service design practice. In 2007, for example, Engine redesigned the service experience for customers in Virgin Atlantic Terminal 3 at London's Heathrow Airport. But, rather than start at the airport, they considered the interactions between customers and Virgin *before* the airport—including how consumers choose and purchase tickets, and how they travel to the airport. Then, at the airport, they redesigned components such as wayfinding systems, check-in procedures, departure lounges, aircraft interiors, as well as the exit from the aircraft and airport.

By considering design across this holistic experience of a passenger, the designers could carefully reconsider the various physical and intangible touchpoints to design a more continuous and coherent service. As well as mapping the customer perspective, Engine's service journey map also mapped staff processes and behaviors for both front- and back-stage staff. Rather than create an entirely new terminal, the designers worked across branding, interiors, products, and service design in order to redesign the systems and touchpoints from a customer perspective.

As opposed to financial or management consultants whose main focus tends to be income maximization, a service design consultancy approach, such as the airline passenger example, is based on improving the customer's experience. Not surprisingly, service design started to be recognized as a valuable opportunity and a means to improve fragmented or incoherent service provisions, particularly across large organizations such as banks or governments (which we will return to in Chapter 6). Large financial and management consultancies such as McKinsey, Deloitte, and Accenture began to incorporate service design into their offerings by either establishing their own specialized sections or buying existing consultancies.[9]

Still a developing field, service design has also incorporated anthropological approaches that might better connect services with people's everyday lives. This can take the form of interviews, questionnaires, or focus groups with all stakeholders involved in a service—not only customers, but also understanding how staff operate and how a new service might impact them. While such research can provide valuable insights, it is also both time-consuming and costly, and tends to be under-valued in the fast-paced corporate realm. After initial research into the service system, designers test possible solutions using mock-ups, prototypes, and role-play scenarios to ensure that the various components of a new service will work before it is implemented on a larger scale.

Although well-placed to consider the customer, service designers and management (to whom they are ultimately beholden) often treat staff as an interchangeable or at least malleable component within a service system. To create a consistent, uniform service, staff may need to play a very specific role, determined by scripts, dress code, behavior modification, and detailed performance instructions. As the McDonald's worker can be seen as just another cog in the system, in new services, staff may be just as interchangeable, and in some cases, even more burdened with the constant demands of role-playing. This issue can be addressed by the inclusion of staff perspectives within a service system. In this scenario, designers may act as facilitators or mediators as much as visualizers—encouraging participation, moderating or stimulating discussion, gathering and filtering themes, as well as developing and refining concepts.

Sharing

The provision of infrastructure, trains, buses, and staff by government agencies to create local, regional, or national public transport systems is an example of service systems that have been around for a long time. In some cases, such as Manhattan, for example, citizens can live, work, and play without owning a car, bicycle, or other means of mobility due to the availability of such systems and the population density. Similarly, car rental agencies have long offered the service of using a car for a short time then returning it, then renting it to someone else. But the rise of the so-called sharing economy in which people interact in a peer-to-peer marketplace facilitated by online applications is seen by some as heralding a new wave of service innovations. Apps like Uber, TaskRabbit, RelayRides, and Mechanical Turk suggest that many of the products we use can be converted into service systems.

The potential of such sharing economy models is a new attitude toward physical things, an "asset-light" life, with less personally owned things and more access to shared things. While a radical change toward a broad "sharing economy" across all aspects of everyday life may or may not eventuate, for now, the model has spread from well-known ride-share and home-share apps such as Uber and Airbnb to a host of meal-sharing, clothes-sharing, and knowledge-sharing apps. Of course, this idea is not entirely new. Sharing a ride to work with a neighbor or borrowing a book from the local library have been everyday practices for many people for decades. One difference is that twenty-first century services are increasingly expected to be on-demand: what if I need to be at work before my neighbor or want a book at midnight when the library is closed?

Launched in San Francisco in 2010 as an alternative cab service, Uber is often portrayed as a pioneer in the disruptive sharing economy (see Case Study 8). In 2012, UberX began to offer a peer-to-peer ride-sharing service, which allowed any car owner to use the app to pick up passengers. Lyft began in the same year, but Uber quickly gained momentum across the United States and around the world. For customers, the new ride-sharing services offered everyone access to a personal car service with a simple mobile interface and cash-free transactions. Uber made the process of connecting real-time moving vehicles and passengers appear simple with its app. As it loads, the user's location is detected via GPS, available drivers are visually displayed on a real-time map, all of which reduces effort on the part of the passenger as location is automatically detected and prices determined.

For drivers, operating in a blurry space between contractor and employee, such apps manage the relationship with the passenger. Uber is careful to avoid use of the word "taxi" so as to avoid legislation or regulations around the existing industry. Legally, Uber tries to maintain no responsibility for accidents or incidents that occur in their service—they claim to be facilitating matches between passengers and drivers (rather than employees). But, while the taxi industry remained regulated, ride-share companies did not need to comply to the same regulations. For taxi companies, auto insurance, criminal background checks, and vehicle inspections all cost money, but ride-share services effectively avoid these, shifting such responsibilities onto the driver.

The transparency of the app's two agents, the passenger and driver may result in a safer experience, as neither is anonymous as in taxis. Interestingly, it seems that all users and drivers are not the same. Shebah, a ride-share service founded in Australia by Georgina McEncroe offered the first all-female ride-share service for drivers and passengers. For women, "McEncroe says one of the most common bits of feedback she gets from her passengers about Shebah is that they can finally sit in the front seat of the car—like men do."[10] The need for such a service confirms that gender biases and social exclusions happen just as much in services of the sharing economy as in any other. As with any designed products, services are not neutral, and universal models always create some kind of exclusion.

A service-based approach to shared resources could replace ownership, so that, with the advent of ride-sharing, an expensive product like a car is no longer necessary for each individual. This may be a more efficient use of existing resources, create a renewed sense of community, and could possibly make services more accessible to low-income people. At least in theory, such platforms could enable non-profit collectives or cooperatives, structured as barter economies or (old-fashioned) sharing systems. But, in practice, sharing costs money. In American cites, popular ride-sharing options such as Uber and Lyft are an additional option for the wealthy who can afford on-demand services while the poor remain reliant on an increasingly underfunded public transport system.

Overall, the sharing economy relies on an available, on-demand workforce engaged in precarious, unprotected work. On the upside, enterprising individuals can offer services through various apps within flexible schedules and without working for an employer. But, free of labor regulations, sharing economy apps are typically designed with payment rates, productivity, and labor conditions controlled by the app owner, limiting the agency of service providers. Service models of access without ownership and on-demand services also rely on a certain scale. Maintaining a pool of available share cars or pool of share tools many may not work in a small town or remote village. The provision of small-scale service design platforms may well be the next challenge for designers.

CASE STUDY 8: UBER

"Where to?" asks the Uber interface, inviting its user to type in a location. The interface's simple design includes up-front fares and estimated arrival time, which allows users to choose a driver and car, and prompts users with shortcuts to previous and frequent destinations. During the ride, the user can continue to use the app to access additional information about their destination, listen to music, or order a meal from a restaurant's menu. Uber offers users a VIP life on-demand. But all services rely on people, and the relationship between users, drivers, and the app maker is a complex one (Figure 11).

FIGURE 11 *A woman passing by an Uber advertisement in Kuala Lumpur, Malaysia, 2018. Getty Images/Faris Hadzig/SOPA Images/Lightrocket.*

In 2014, 4,000 London cabs brought the center of London to a standstill, following similar protests in Paris, Madrid, Rome, Milan, and Berlin. Uber's service was subsequently banned in Germany, and in 2017 London's transport regulator rejected Uber's application to renew its operating license in the city. While for some, this was the last gasp of a disrupted taxi industry, a range of issues emerged from such actions, including driver working conditions, congestion, and pollution. Uber had disrupted not only the taxi industry but also mobility in general as its ease of use discourages alternatives such as public transport, cycling, or walking.[11]

The app also changes the nature of work for drivers. Unlike other online marketplace apps, the service providers (drivers) do not get to set the price for their service. Uber sets prices using an opaque "surge pricing" algorithm so that price surges occur at times of peak demand in popular locations. Uber collects payment through the app directly at the time of a journey's completion, yet pays drivers weekly, and drivers must pay gas, insurance, and maintenance on their cars. As contractors rather than employees, legal working conditions and minimum wage regulations do not apply.

Behind the interface, the app not only sets prices and collects payments, but also functions as a management tool that produces "on-demand labour."[12] Gamification techniques in the form of regular notifications and reward badges for drivers who reach certain milestones, as well as motivation and enticements to keep working have led to accusations of psychological manipulation. The "star rating" system to rate driver performance also functions as a form of performance management and surveillance, as drivers are not only expected to drive safely but also engage in social interaction to ensure good ratings. This "emotional" labor is another hidden cost of the sharing economy and the service industry more generally.

Hackathons and jams

Collaborative events and the sharing of tools, techniques, and knowledge both in person and online are defining characteristics of new approaches to design, particularly in new fields such as service design. In the absence of formal education, various informal means of acquiring knowledge and skills cater to emerging service designers. A range of activities and toolkits—from envisaging and prototyping tools to graphs and games—are freely available online. Designed to aid practitioners in creating service blueprints and customer experience journeys, such resources are also beginning to establish a common language and a familiar set of techniques. Although they tend to over-use alliteration, overviews such as the "Double Diamond"—"Discover, Define, Develop, Deliver"—recommended by the British Design Council's Service Design Guide, provide useful frameworks.[13]

Design jams and hackathons are an essential part of this new phenomenon. A hackathon (a hacking marathon), originally referred to an event in which computer programmers aimed to develop collaborative ideas in an intensive, short period of time.[14] Typically organized around a particular project, the idea was to encourage experimentation and innovation, and the events ranged from informal pizza parties to formal corporate and competitive events with funding opportunities and prizes. During the 2000s, the idea spread to other industries who generally used "jam" to describe such events. Like a musical jam session, such events implied an informal setting in which to generate new ideas, practice, or experiment with new techniques.

A design jam also involves collaboration, experimentation, and often involves an element of competition. Jams run over a specified period—from two hours to two days—and are open to designers and non-designers, professionals, and amateurs. Framed around a particular challenge or problem with constraints, a design jam provides a platform for participants to workshop ideas (particularly experimental ideas), develop networks, and work collaboratively. Participants break up into groups to brainstorm and discuss ideas, prioritize them and choose the best, then sketch, storyboard, or flowchart their solution, receive feedback, refine, and finalize. With the 2011 Global Service Jam drawing 1,200 participants from fifty cities, design jams are now addressing large-scale issues drawn from government services, transportation, health, and urban development.

But the design jam's fast-paced covering of whiteboards with post-it notes, sketches of service journey maps, cardboard interface prototypes, and enthusiastic idea pitches represent only the beginning of a complex design process. Realistically, participants are unlikely to come up with solutions for redesigning a city's healthcare services in two hours or halting climate change in a day. Their urgency and emphasis on immediate action are also at odds with the slowness of user research and understanding diverse viewpoints.

Community and user input are either minimal or absent entirely, resulting in design processes secluded from the world by participants with the means to attend. In short, hackathons and jams emphasize "quick and forceful action with socially similar collaborators over the contestations of mass democracy or the slow construction of coalition across difference."[15] Although resulting in prototypes or maps or plans, the participants rarely have an opportunity to implement their resulting design solutions. But, as collaborative processes, educational opportunities and inspirational events—particularly when hackathons and jams bring together a diverse range of participants—the filtering, discussion, and refining processes are a useful, if limited, introduction to design.

Social design

If designers ultimately aim to improve human well-being, some designers involved in systems and services have utilized their skills to specifically address social problems. As opposed to market-driven design practice, social design is devoted to solving particular social problems and typically adopts a systemic or services-based approach. From alleviating poverty and homelessness to creating new educational opportunities or healthy food options, social design aims to generate positive social impact and sustainability. Rather than beginning with an idea for a new product or a new system, social designers are concerned with a holistic process in which community participation is vital.

A design project led by Ezio Manzini and François Jégou, Sustainable Everyday, illustrates this approach. The project, which culminated in a 2003 exhibition in Milan and a book, *Sustainable Everyday: Scenarios of Urban Life*, had a significant impact. Sustainable Everyday aimed at creating proposals and alternative scenarios for sustainable living. Working with people's everyday experiences, the design approach is based on a "bottom-up" strategy that operates on various micro scales. Examples included the question: "How can we have a more sustainable and practical, daily management of food activities?" One scenario was a "Kitchen Club," an ongoing collaboration within an apartment building where members order shopping that is delivered in bulk, then stored and prepared in a common kitchen, and costs are shared via a pay-per-use system.[16]

Other examples, from communal laundry systems to transport-sharing and tool-sharing systems tended toward small scale, sustainable uses of existing resources, infrastructure, and systems. Importantly, social design aims to benefit people, but includes the end users in designing solutions. As opposed to the fast-paced, designer-driven hackathon model, social design typically involves a slower, inclusive process that creates a platform for community input and collaboration. It is thus social as it facilitates people to participate in designing their own future scenarios, ensuring that the users of a new service or system are intimately involved in the design process. As a "bottom-up" approach, community participants therefore have a greater sense of ownership over the completed design solution.

While service design is usually associated with developed economies with strong service sectors, Indian designer and educator Singanapalli Balaram's concept of "Invisible Design" considers the role of services within a developing country.[17] Balaram envisages the designer's role in poor communities in India as one extending beyond discrete products to instead become a documenter, community facilitator, activist, and integrator—all framed within participatory and user-centered models of design practice. What Balaram describes as invisible design does not begin with the idea of design as a means to increase corporate competitive advantage but involves social interventions embedded within communities.

Within low-income and indigenous communities, foreign products, systems, and services may not be understood, appropriate, or needed. In "top-down" models, global corporations seeking new markets for their products or distant governments establishing services often fail to achieve their desired results. In contrast, existing examples of micro-finance cooperatives in India or mobile phone sharing initiatives in Africa work within local cultural and social contexts. On a larger scale, an initiative such as RITA, the Indigenous Tourism Network of Mexico, is a good example of a more grass-roots approach to systems and service design. RITA promotes sustainable, indigenous tourism experiences in Mexico via a collaborative network of village micro-businesses, government agencies, and global organizations. Importantly, it is led and run by indigenous communities, and combines software design, administrative and promotional services to enable tourists to engage with indigenous knowledge of particular environments, local cuisines, and ancient sites and stories.[18]

Social design has gained traction over the last two decades, particularly with the new possibilities enabled by new technologies. Shrinking government services and support platforms in many countries also means local communities need to take more of a role in their own service provisions. In this sense, people need to design their own lives more than ever before. Whether we like it or not, service design of the future may require everyone to be a designer. But, while Manzini argues that everyone is potentially a designer, our innate design capacity "must be stimulated and cultivated."[19] Education clearly plays a role in this, but so does the kind of participation and co-creation engendered by social design.

But an ongoing difficultly and future challenge for designers in this area is how to measure or assess social impact? While conventional product design can be measured in units sold or profit taken, the aim of social design is very different and the effects of a given service are difficult to measure. The time horizon of many social design projects is often much longer than, say, a corporate service that needs to be designed and implemented quickly. And, for designers typically trained in analysis, visualization, and communication, additional skills in facilitation, mediation, and team-building are essential in building an effective social design practice. Despite these challenges, collaborative and participatory approaches to design may become more common with recent developments in active citizenship and debates about the design of public services.

Government services

In most countries, the public sector is responsible for the largest and most diverse range of services. Governments provide services for the broadest range of people across different timescales. These include ongoing healthcare and law and order services, periodic services such as collecting taxes and census data, and long-term services such as designing and constructing infrastructure projects like highways and power plants. Many of these services directly impact citizens, who not only participate by voting for particular political parties, but also participate in co-creating government services. Unlike some of the examples we have seen above, government service provisions are usually on a large scale, involving millions of citizens. In the public sector, governments have turned to design and to service designers in particular to aid in better delivering their services.

Over the past two decades, local, regional, and national governments have had to respond to digitalization and new platforms for their services. As large-scale public utilities, government services are incredibly varied and rarely uniform, or standardized. And, as most government institutions were created in the pre-digital era, services are typically siloed in public service departments without any cohesion or consistency, often resulting in frustration for citizens. To start a new business, for example, may involve dealing with three or four separate government departments for the appropriate applications, permits, and permissions, all of them designed differently. Service design within government not only aims to provide citizens with more efficient and universal access to services, but can also save resources for governments too.

Since 2011, the UK's Government Digital Service (GDS), operating as part of the government rather than an external agency, has been leading the digitization of government services. Their Gov.UK website combined all of the national government's various departmental websites onto a single platform, now accessed by millions of people daily. The GDS team of graphic, service, and interaction designers led by the UK Government Director of Design, Louise Downe, then focused specifically on design for government services in a more holistic way. Launched in 2018, the GOV.UK Design System enabled coherent, consistent interfaces across government services—from layout and typography to interactive websites and standard payment systems—this systematized approach included a service standard manual and code of practice.

Although such service design practice in government is not as well developed in the United States at the federal or state level, the New York City Mayor's office includes a Service Design Studio. One of their first major projects was the redesign of ACCESS NYC in 2017, a website for services for the 20 percent of New York's population who live in poverty, many of whom were not getting the services and benefits available to them.[20] The site was redesigned and launched in simple English and six additional languages (four more added in 2018), simplifying the processes and options. This involved streamlining inputs from over fifteen Federal, State, and City agencies into a unified visual system and language, accessible and clear for citizens.

For government at all levels, key principles of the digital economy and on-demand accessibility are now expected by their citizens. Increasing government services' transparency, efficiency, and the personalization of services are also ongoing design issues. Given governments are usually the largest providers of services in any country, how they are designed impacts millions of people, so that even slight changes may require careful research, analysis, and redesign. And the last problem for designers working within government is the fact that services are constantly changing due to not only changes in technology, but also changes in government policy that may increase or decrease resources available for certain services.

Conclusion

Services are particularly dynamic. Unlike designing a chair or a logo, service design never reaches a stable solution. And, given the variety of people interacting with service touchpoints, a uniform or standardized approach to every aspect is rarely appealing. For some, a future direction of service design lies in increasingly personalized services via a variety of apps that can sort through the range of available options, prices, availability, or ratings that are all compared to personal profiles and preferences. The ideal may be an increase of personal services on-demand, all the time, delivered in an efficient manner. For others, the approach of social designers or those designing government services suggests that future scenarios inevitably involve other people. In this case, collaborative, community-based, co-designed solutions offer an alternative way forward.

Chapter summary

- PSS mix tangible and intangible things
- A systemic approach to design considers discrete products within larger systems

- A new discipline "service design" is devoted to designing better services
- Social design encourages user participation and co-creation in the design process
- Governments, the biggest providers of services, are increasingly turning to design

5

Experiences

As we process information on a screen, handle our new smartphone, or navigate its systems, we experience emotions. Our interactions with information, products, systems, and services are mediated by our senses and memories, as well as our intellect. Our experience might be characterized by pleasure, satisfaction, frustration, or disappointment, or a combination of these. We not only perceive what things might do for us, but also filter our interactions through sight and sound, touch and smell, through our nervous and muscular systems, as well as through our memories and desires. Not surprisingly, designers are increasingly interested in this aspect of a user's interactions with designed artifacts.

Designers attentive to user experiences typically engage in research to determine not only how designed things enable people to perform useful functions, but also how they affect users' emotions. In order to better understand users, the usual design practices of prototyping, iteration, and user scenarios are supplemented by interviews, surveys, diary studies, and lab-based research in collaboration with psychologists, sociologists, or anthropologists. Ultimately, design for experience draws upon all of the concepts we have covered in this book so far. It is fundamentally interdisciplinary and can include physical and virtual experiences as well as the interactions between them.

Interaction and emotion

Industrial, mass-produced things have always been marketed, advertised, and branded in emotional terms. While some designers in the twentieth century remained fixated on utility as the only aim of good design, others understood that our interaction with products elicits emotional responses. We buy products not only for what they do but also for how they make us feel. From the satisfaction of using a well-designed tool to the frustration of struggling to find information on a new website, our emotional response to designed things is an essential facet of any product, system, or service. And, although designers often strive for innovative solutions, radical disruptions may not be as successful for users as gradual, incremental changes.

In his 1951 autobiography, industrial designer Raymond Loewy summed up what he believed to be a designer's key to commercial success. Loewy's design career included numerous iconic designs, from the Coca-Cola bottle and Exxon logo to streamlined Greyhound buses and Frigidaire ovens. His MAYA, or "Most Advanced Yet Acceptable" principle, proposed that the new product with the best prospects for success was novel yet still recognizable to the public.[1] Designers should aim for a balance between novelty and familiarity, so that a new product should not be so novel that consumers could not comprehend what it was or how it worked. Ultimately, MAYA implied gradual changes could ease user's fear of the new yet still stimulate curiosity.

Loewy's principle has become standard in the design of many contemporary products, interactions, and services. Netflix and Spotify, for example, offer personalized selections of new movies and songs that are similar to ones that users have seen and heard before. Rather than long lists of unfamiliar titles that might be intimidating or overwhelming, their algorithms compile music and videos that are new but familiar (epitomized by the "because you liked" lists). Spotify's "Discover Weekly" function offers listeners a personalized list of new music, but always includes a familiar band or song. Popular films and TV series use a similar strategy with ongoing franchises, spin-off series, and sequels. In some instances, rather than form, form follows familiarity.

Interestingly, the most familiar designs are not always the most functional. The QWERTY keyboard, for example, became standard in the late nineteenth century when the manufacturer Remington used it to solve a problem in typewriter design. The vowels, as the most used keys, needed to be spaced out on a typewriter keyboard so that the mechanical rods attached to the keys would not stick to each other when typing quickly. The QWERTY layout solved that particular problem. But then it became so familiar with users that it continued on computer keyboards that do not use mechanical keys. Although designers have since developed more intuitive and functional keyboards that enable faster typing, QWERTY's familiarity has consistently won out over proposed changes.[2]

More typically, designs change incrementally over time, ensuring a balance between novelty and familiarity. The software programs within Microsoft Office, for example, have changed substantially since the 1980s, yet each iteration represented a series of small changes, while basic functions remained familiar. As a suite of programs, Microsoft Word, Excel, and PowerPoint maintained the same interface, ensuring familiarity for users. Their menus, toolbars, buttons, and tabs remained consistent with each upgrade, even as new features as spell checking or mobile versions added to the functions. Radical change can lead to frustration, as users expect to quickly adapt to a new version rather than spend hours learning a new interface, commands, or structure.

To understand design from an emotional perspective, psychological researchers analyze not only the functional use of designed artifacts, but also users' sensory interactions such as sight, sound, and touch, as well as non-physical interactions such as desires or memories. Psychologists Paul Hekkert and Hendrik N. J. Schifferstein identified three main components of user experience of a product.[3] First, an aesthetic response based on a user's sensory perception of a product (its look, feel, or sound); second, its functional value based on which actions it affords and how it is operated; and last, the expressive, symbolic, or mythological associations people have with a product. They also note that the context in which our interactions take place is important—the atmosphere of the environment in which our interaction occurs can impact on our experience.

Hospitals, for example, can be particularly stressful environments and designers working in a health context are trying to understand how to create better experiences and interactions with medical equipment and services. Dedicated to improving patient experiences, Philips Healthcare Ambient Experience has pioneered a holistic design approach. While Philips had long designed innovative healthcare products, this initiative shifted their emphasis from products to experiences. Like other healthcare manufacturers, Philips traditionally concentrated on designing faster, more precise medical imaging systems such as MRI (Magnetic Resonance Imaging) and CT (Computed Tomography) scanners, as this is what radiologists and medical specialists requested. But no one considered the patient's perspective.

After years of research and development, the Ambient Experience program was launched in 2007 in an attempt to improve the patient's experience. Led by designer Stefano Marzano, Philips Design refocused from a technology-driven to a user-centered design philosophy. Rather than improving imaging devices, they focused on the patient experience, particularly how to relax a patient in a potentially stressful situation. The Philips team discovered that "the level of stress of the patient is affected not only by what happens during the exam but also *before* and *after* the exam, and in particular by the *environment* in which the entire experience takes place."[4] For their research, they drew on a wide variety of expertise, including interior and industrial designers, sociologists, and psychologists, as well as clinical staff.

In order to soothe anxiety in patients, the newly designed clinical environment included video wall projections, a dynamic lighting and audio system, and clear and efficient spaces for clinical staff. In order to alleviate the feeling of patient isolation, it included visual communication between the patient, staff, and family in the next room via video cameras. Beyond the examination room, the design team also considered the patient experience before and after scanning. Children, for example, often find MRI and CT machines frightening, and in some cases need to be sedated to ensure they stay still inside them. The designers included a scaled down version of a scanner in the waiting room, making the machine more familiar to children. Finally, patients were considered as participants in the experience, as they choose their own lighting, visual, and audio themes, giving them a sense of control.

One of the essential issues in considering emotional responses and experiences is that they are, by definition, subjective. Not only will every person experience products and situations differently, but experiences are also different according to gender, age, education, cultural, and social background. How to design for such a variety of individual experiences can seem overwhelming, particularly when the demands of mass production and mass consumerism encourage standardization and uniform approaches to design. But, in what is becoming an evolving field devoted to creating meaningful experiences for users, designers are creating numerous possibilities for flexible interactions with products and services.

The shift from mass advertising to personalized messaging, for example, is creating more dynamic, compelling advertising across digital media platforms such as social media, news channels, and search engines. Created via algorithms that collate real-time data, individual purchase histories, and preferences, advertisers can now deliver more personally targeted messages rather than campaigns designed for an ideal or generic user. For now, such interactions are primarily one-sided (with consumers having little choice or input), yet future applications promise more personalized content, searches, media, and experiences. Here, the inclusion of users not only as research data but also as part of the design process is an important next step.

Participation and co-creation

As we saw in the last chapter, a significant issue in the design of early computing technology was the gap between specialist technicians and non-specialist end users. Computer scientists and engineers developed the new technological tools in research labs, and then installed mainframe computers and systems in workplaces. As HCI developed, designers began to focus on users and their interaction with the technology. Yet computer engineers and software designers typically remained focused on functionality, efficiency and optimal performance. But in Scandinavia, a different approach to designing new technologies had a major impact—rather than design new technologies *for* users, the idea was to design *with* users.

In 1972, computer scientist Kristen Nygaard began a project with the Norwegian Iron and Metal Workers Union to develop techniques by which to work directly with users. Involving users in the design process, particularly for complex computer systems, was a radical step, but Nygaard's project inspired other computer scientists who initiated similar projects in Sweden and Denmark. The best-known, called UTOPIA, led by Pelle Ehn, aimed for user participation in all phases of the design and development of computer systems and tools.[5] Developed with the Nordic Graphic Union, as the industry was becoming digitized in the early 1980s, UTOPIA was conceived partly as a means to integrate existing craft skills into new software development. Its "Future Workshops" enabled workers, designers, and researchers to design solutions oriented toward a better future for all.

The benefits of such an approach include improved user knowledge of workplace tools and systems, easier implementation of new technologies or techniques, less resistance to change, and increased communication and collaboration. What was distinctive about the Scandinavian model was the idea of increasing workplace democracy through workers' participation in designing their future. In this model, new technologies were recast as resources to enable better work rather than efficient systems imposed from above to save time or money. Broad economic and political changes over the last two decades of the twentieth century, including globalized production, weakening of union power, and a devaluing of industrial labor resulted in difficulties implementing such participatory design models. Additionally, the prevalence of off-the-shelf computer products and systems meant the ideals of worker-developed technologies all but disappeared by the early twenty-first century.

But in other ways, participatory design spread from Scandinavia via information technology and product design communities. Rather than based in unions and labor organizations, it shifted in the United States context to align more with user-trials to ensure the commercial success of new technologies. While still rooted in computing and software design, participatory design has had a significant impact in other fields over the past thirty years and manifest in various ways. In design fields, such as architecture and urban planning, for example, public participation has increased due to a traditional lack of consultation in designing public spaces and infrastructure. The idea that the public should have an active role in planning decisions has been a recurring refrain since the 1960s.

Importantly, participatory design highlights the idea of the designer-user relationship as a reciprocal and ongoing one, and design as a fundamentally collaborative endeavor. Participatory design also situates dialogue and negotiation at the center of the design process, which is not always a comfortable position for a traditional designer who relied on intuition and individual creativity. Methods such as user workshops with prototype objects or environments, games, role-playing, or scenarios, as well as sketches or models that engage users through a "hands on" experience continue to be developed as means by which users can participate and contribute.

While productive, such techniques also have limitations. First, users do not always know what the problems are or the best ways to fix them. Second, designers need to function as facilitators as much as creators. This may require a significant amount of translation between users or groups—the language and practices of healthcare clinicians, for example, is very different to the language and practices of computer engineers. And, ultimately, final decisions about not only the way forward but also how to implement it need to be agreed upon by all parties. Again, the designer's role may shift to negotiator or diplomat to ensure that an outcome is finally achieved.

Drawing upon the legacy of participatory design, researchers have argued that contemporary practice is blurring the roles of designer, user, and researcher.[6] Co-design or co-creation, like participatory design, requires some relinquishing of control of design and development to users. It also requires thinking of users as active participants rather than passive consumers. Although the designer's role could potentially be diminished within this model, designers still play a critical role due to their visual thinking and research skills. But design for individual needs may not correspond to collective needs—that is, how can we co-design not only for a singular user but also for a larger community?

Creative Commons projects are examples of large-scale participatory or co-design practices that allow users to use, improve, and share design ideas online. Such projects rely on a model of collective innovation and collaboration rather than individual or corporate intellectual property and patents. Linux is a good example of an ongoing, large-scale user innovation project. Initially released in 1991 by Finnish software engineer Linus Thorvalds, Linux comprises an open-source operating system and software applications whose underlying code can be modified and distributed. In another way, social media enables certain new forms of participation and co-creation—Facebook (see Case Study 9), Instagram, and Twitter all facilitate the distribution of ideas and collaborative projects on a global scale.

Another example of user-driven participatory design process is one driven by "lead users" who develop or modify existing products that are later commercialized for a mass audience. This has occurred in fields as diverse as surgical equipment, library information systems, and sporting equipment.[7] In the latter, "extreme" sports people often experiment with new techniques or modify products to fulfill their own particular needs, then these become more widespread as others adopt and modify them. Such innovations developed by users are occasionally adopted by manufacturers and proceed to mass production. Contrary to the assumption that only designers and manufacturers create novel designs, users also innovate and contribute to design processes.

More public design outcomes such as national graphics, community logos, or emblems have also incorporated user participation, to greater and lesser degrees of success. In 2015, for example, the New Zealand Government opened a competition for a new national flag. To replace the existing flag, based on the (British) Union Jack and Southern Cross, New Zealand citizens were invited to submit designs that embodied the country's distinctive cultural values. The resulting designs ranged from stylized Maori "koru" designs (based on unfurling fern fronds) to kiwi birds. In all, the Flag Consideration Project panel received 10,292 designs, which they reduced to a shortlist of four which were then voted by the public into a single option. But, in the final referendum, the New Zealand public voted to stick with the old flag.

Similarly, the design of the Tokyo 2020 Olympics logo was subject to public participation after the original logo was withdrawn after plagiarism accusations. An Olympic logo design competition was then open to the Japanese public. Out of 15,000 entries received by the Tokyo Olympics committee, artist Asao Tokolo's "harmonized chequered emblem," a blue geometric pattern based on a traditional design, won. Although popular with the public, examples of participation such as the New Zealand flag and Tokyo Olympics competitions promoted the AIGA, America's preeminent professional design organization, to publish an open letter, "Against Crowdsourcing Logo Design." Such a participatory approach, they argued, undermines design's collaborative engagement, fee structure, and professional experience.[8]

This tension between professional designers and co-creating users may be resolved by redefining the designers' role as closer to a facilitator rather than a creator. This would require a significant shift in design education and professional practice, but there are signs that such a shift is already underway. Among the various co-creation and participatory methods currently available, educator and designer Elizabeth Sanders's MakeTools consultancy has created useful toolkits for co-design and participatory design.[9] Interestingly, their vocabulary extends beyond a traditional designers', utilizing terms such as dreaming, feeling, mapping, remembering, storytelling, and visioning as means to discover users' needs and understand their experiences.

A final new approach, based on combining user-centered and participatory design ideas, is the living lab. A living lab operates within existing communities and settings such as medical facilities, aged care facilities, or educational spaces. Such labs allow for an immersive experience for users and a space for designing and evaluating their own future scenario. Variations on these living labs have been used to develop new products, services, and policies. As practice-driven spaces, living labs—unlike traditional scientific labs—are working environments where innovative or experimental techniques can be studied and evaluated.[10] In a sense, living labs offer designers a prototyping process on a larger scale than a sketch, yet they are small enough to allow for mistakes before scaling up. Their use is proving popular in projects involving government, corporations, and universities.

CASE STUDY 9: FACEBOOK

Founded in a Harvard dorm room in 2004, Facebook began as an online repository of student profiles and interests, a digital version of paper "facebooks" that some colleges distributed to students. As it grew beyond educational institutions after 2006, Facebook added interactive features such as groups, messaging, timelines, games, and news feeds. The platform's extraordinary growth to over 2 billion active users has resulted in a constantly morphing and complex design.

Facebook facilitates communication with family and friends through posting and sharing information and enables connection to communities of like-minded people (Figure 12). Mobile and accessible on various devices, its consistent labeling, icons, and signature blue and white color palette made digital interaction simple. Organized around a user's personal preferences, the platform also enables user participation and interaction through likes, comments, and replies. Facebook's "like" button, a stylized "thumbs up" icon, and emoji-like "reactions" make social interaction quick and fun.

But Facebook is also designed to entice more use. Notifications in the form of vibrations, sounds, or icons appear on screens to remind users to interact. Emotionally, Facebook quantifies self-validation in the number of "likes" we do (or do not) get on each post. The dynamic content and fear of missing out lead some users feeling permanently "tethered" to the site. Critics, such as The Center for Humane Technology, claim such features are part of a system "designed to addict us."[11]

Like all social media corporations, Facebook is founded on user-generated content. But the technology and algorithms behind the platform are invisible to users. Users' personal data and online behavior (purchases, likes, comments, and website visits) are gathered, compiled into profiles, then sold to advertisers. Masked by ideals of free communication and social relationships, our digitized selves, likes, and relationships are quantified into advertiser-friendly data.

FIGURE 12 *A picture taken in Moscow on March 22, 2018, shows the Russian language version of Facebook about page featuring the face of founder and CEO Mark Zuckerberg. MLADEN ANTONOV/AFP/Getty Images.*

The 2016 US election campaign highlighted another issue. With the addition of News Feeds, Facebook became a dominant media publisher, yet the company persists in promoting their image as a neutral communications platform. Viral fake news stories and fake profiles undermined users' trust. Given its algorithms are generally designed to tailor information to individual likes and preferences, they tend to reinforce users' existing ideas and amplify fear and anger rather than expose users to differing ideas.

Issues of privacy and trust in the platform are paramount, particularly in the wake of the data mining scandal in which Cambridge Analytica gained access to over 80 million users' information and sold this on. In 2018 Congress hearings, Mark Zuckerberg repeatedly insisted that users controlled their data. Yet reports of "shadow profiles" of data gathered from people who had never used Facebook and the CEO's paranoia regarding his own security and privacy also undermined trust.

Despite these issues, Facebook is a corporation that is designing experiences for over 2 billion people. Facebook's design team's facilitation of social action through their recent Social Good tools, such as coordinating disaster relief and identifying personal crises, suggest that it has potential for both individual and collective benefits. But more difficult questions remain, such as how to design for information dissemination without polarization? How far should it shape communities?

Inclusive experience

As we have seen in previous chapters, there is no such thing as an average user. Unfortunately, many aspects of our physical environment, products, systems, and services are designed for one. From childhood to old age, all humans have varied physical and mental abilities across their lifetime, yet designers often make assumptions about an ideal, able body and mind. Individuals also have temporarily changing needs, such as a broken arm or a need for reading glasses, as well as more permanent impairments that require wheelchairs or a guide dog. Indigenous people or those marginalized within a community may experience a very different world from that designed for them by others. Creating inclusive experiences is an essential issue for contemporary designers.

Rather than disabled, researcher Rosemarie Garland-Thomson uses to the term "misfit," suggesting that disability is not only a physical state but also a social condition. In the inextricable link between the two, she writes that the design of our everyday lives "tends to offer fits to majority bodies and functioning and created misfits with minority forms of embodiment." Anyone outside the norm—that is, too far from the average user—is a misfit.[12] Universal Design, Design for All, Inclusive Design all refer to principles for designers, architects, and planners for design that considers the needs of everyone. Designers who have incorporated this approach aim to design environments, products, interactions, and services that are usable by the greatest number of people, regardless of abilities.

Rising global healthcare standards have resulted in people born with impairments, afflicted by serious injuries or illness, and an aging population, are living more active, independent lives. But, as we have seen in previous chapters, universal sizes and standard models create problems for people outside of those "norms," affecting their sense of autonomy, dignity, and engendering feelings of exclusion for people who do not fit. Consider, for example, someone in a wheelchair. Their height affects not only reach ability for a cupboard or workstation but also sight lines for wayfinding systems, while the chair itself requires certain turning circles and environments free from obstructions.

Universal Design principles go back to the 1950s, when Tim Nugent at University of Illinois began the "barrier-free" movement. Beginning with ramps and parking spaces for people using wheelchairs, the idea of making everyday experiences normal for people outside mobility norms stemmed from designers working in the built environment. British architect Selwyn Goldsmith's *Designing for the Disabled*, a 1963 guide to architectural planning for accessibility, included innovations such as the dropped curb, now commonplace in most cities. Architect, designer, and educator Ronald

Mace popularized the term "Universal Design" in the United States as the idea of developing standards and "barrier-free" specifications for the built environment gathered momentum during the 1970s, and moved into product and other design fields (as we saw with Patricia Moore in Chapter 2).

Initially, this entailed adapting or renovating buildings to provide better access, but later Universal Design principles became part of building codes and standards to consider not only doors and stairs but also bathroom facilities and furniture. Progress was slow and ad hoc until the 1990 Americans with Disabilities Act (ADA), which prohibited discrimination and made built environment changes mandatory, at least in new public buildings. By this time, some designers also began addressing how to design more accessible transportation and communication systems, such as bus and train, telephone and computing systems. But the promise of universal access did not live up to the reality of everyday life for many who still struggle in a designed world that continues to create misfits (see Case Study 10).

Another inclusive way of understanding design addresses other communities of "misfits". The idea of decolonizing design began as an initiative to recognize design's ongoing colonial frameworks and reassess indigenous concepts of design, craft, and community. But, in an even more holistic way, decolonization involves reconsidering the relationship between design and the politics of cultural difference. In short, this involves an understanding of alternative modes of modernity. The dominant, Euro-American set of assumptions about design dismisses not only indigenous modes of making, but also indigenous spiritual and knowledge practices. On the level of experiences, this involves acknowledging that indigenous cultures may have radically different values, norms, and users.

Maria Rogal's Design for Development (now Decolonizing Design) projects at the University of Florida, for example, illustrate one aspect of this. Over the past decade, this initiative comprises graphic design students from the United States who collaborate with indigenous people in rural Mexico on projects that aim to bring designers in contact with people without access to professional design. Participatory design in the sense of co-creation and collaboration are essential strategies in working between cultures. The indigenous Mayan people of the Yucatán peninsular, whose culture and way of life has long been suppressed by colonialism, also face contemporary discrimination and the demands of mass tourism for clichéd representations of their culture. The latter includes a tendency for touristic imagery to caricature indigenous cultures as "primitive" without any understanding of their modern lives.

Rogal and her students address the problem of how to help develop services, products, or tourist experiences that will generate income for indigenous people without compromising their culture. For the American designers, essential issues such as building trust and partnerships, sharing information, and granting agency to indigenous people to maintain control of how they are represented are key to the design process. Furthermore, the respect for indigenous knowledge—from their relationship to the environment, rituals, language, medicines, cosmology, spiritual beliefs, and varied histories—is crucial. For professional designers, a decolonial method includes "suspending judgment and surrendering the belief that they knew, in advance, anything meaningful about the people with whom they were working."[13] The humility inherent in this approach acknowledges not only differing frames of reference, but also different ways of experiencing the world.

Today, designers and activists working to decolonize design are questioning the foundations of much contemporary design practice and thinking.[14] The knowledge systems, categories, definitions, and standards of professional design are typically framed as Euro-American and white. In this way, colonial foundations and frameworks have become global standards and assumptions that impose specific norms and values on varied cultures throughout the world. Our envisaged future—its designed systems, services, and experiences—continues to be designed from a perspective that tends to assimilate everyone into a singular world-view. Instead, advocates of decolonial design propose disruption via alternative practices that enable a plurality of world-views.

CASE STUDY 10: UNIVERSAL DESIGN

The most recognizable symbol of inclusion, the International Symbol of Access (ISA), is composed of a blue square with a stylized white figure in a wheelchair. It was designed in 1968 by Danish design student Susanne Koefoed. Adopted and adapted by Rehabilitation International and later by governments and the United Nations, the ISA became a standard symbol found in airports, hospitals, and bathrooms. It spread globally through the 1970s and 1980s on public signage, transport systems, parks, museums, and educational facilities.

The ISA's short history is a compelling case study of the changes in attitude toward inclusion over the past fifty years. During the fight for access by disability activists in the 1970s, for example, the ISA became more than just a wayfinding device, it became a symbol of identity, "a unifying icon of protest."[15] Yet for some, it remained controversial—was it a symbol of inclusion or of segregation?

In 2010, Sara Hendren and Brian Glenney launched the Accessible Icon Project, to promote an alternative icon. Designed by Tim Ferguson Sauder, the new icon is similar to the ISA, yet the figure appears dynamic. Rather than a static, helpless figure in a wheelchair, it conveys the idea that people with impairments are dynamic and able. While it has not been accepted as a global standard, the project provoked considerable discussion on accessibility and inclusion. Yet, even this new version is problematic, suggested critics, as the vast majority of people categorized under the ADA as "disabled" do not actually use wheelchairs.

Meanwhile, product designers have also turned their attention to inclusive design. Most notably Smart Design's OXO Good Grips range of kitchen utensils. Launched in 1990, the original Good Grips range was conceived as better tools specifically for people with arthritis—yet their non-slip, comfortable handles proved popular with everyone. Smart Design's more recent home products, developed in collaboration with biomechanical researchers, ensure ease of use by the greatest number of people.

Interactive designers working with new technologies have also developed inclusive tools. On the one hand, this means ensuring interfaces and devices are accessible, and on the other, it means developing assistive technologies that aid people with specific needs. The former includes alternatives to text (such as audio) and navigation (keyboards, mouse use, or screen use). The latter includes vision and hearing impairment simulation software and dexterity simulator gloves that help designers assess the visual clarity of websites or the operability of machines.

Maximum inclusion is vital for designing things used by large populations, particularly something as commonplace as money. The new British ten-pound note, for example, a colorful polymer note with braille-like raised dots in the top-left corner, was designed in collaboration with the Royal National Institute for the Blind (Figure 13). Designing for equitable use—designing things that require low

FIGURE 13 *A cluster of raised dots, a tactile feature to help the visually impaired, sit on the new UK 10-pound banknote, 2017. Getty Images: Credit: Bloomberg.*

physical effort, are simple and intuitive to use, and have a flexibility that allows for various users and abilities—has become less a specialized design field and more of an issue of adhering to basic human rights.

The experience economy

Just before the turn of the century, economists Joseph Pine and James Gilmore wrote an account of the importance of experience that drew the attention of business and marketing executives. In "Welcome to the Experience Economy," they stated that, in the future, goods and services will no longer be the leading economic drivers, but "staging experiences" would be the new driver of economic growth.[16] As distinct from goods, services, and interactions, they argued, experiences are engaging, memorable, and personal. Creating a compelling experience for businesses required designing a coherent set of "cues" such as interior décor, uniforms, and signage, and eliminating distractions from the theme. In short, designing engaging sensory stimulations was the key to future economic prosperity.

As proof, Pine and Gilmore noted the rise in scripted scenes, staged activities, and curated ambiences across a variety of retail industries. Borrowing from theme parks and casinos, the idea of designing experiences certainly spread across retail and service industries to education and government agencies in the first two decades of the twenty-first century. From cultural festivals to historic precincts, nations, regions, and cities began to market themselves via experiences to attract not only tourists but also businesses and migrants. Social media has proven an ideal platform for documenting and sharing experiences so that the Facebook vacation destination or Instagramable restaurant filter our consumption of real spaces and products. And designers are increasingly attuned to creating environments and props that can be absorbed into such experiences.

Although hotels have long been devoted to delivering services, a new wave of boutique hotels in the 1980s and 1990s highlighted the idea of creating unique experiences. In California, Bill Kimpton's Kimpton Hotels and Chip Conley's Joie de Vivre group began renovated and converted old hotels into boutique experiences with an emphasis on service, individuality, and fine dining. Contrary to the luxury chain hotels that offered generic experiences throughout the globe, the boutique hotel offered an idiosyncratic experience, related to its particular place, services, or ambience. This idea of hotels with a distinctive "personality" was perhaps best exemplified by the New York hotels of hotelier Ian Schrager in partnership with designer Philippe Starck. Together, their renovations of the Royalton, the Paramount, and the Hudson redesigned the hotel experience for a young, globetrotting, and fashion-conscious clientele who were bored with generic hotel experiences.

The Royalton set the scene. From the exterior, there was little to suggest a hotel. Underplayed signage and subtle cues (such as a snake-like banister) confirmed the idea that you needed to be "in the know" to find it. Inside, guests entered a long space, a royal-blue rug with a curious snake and bird motif extending its length. A mahogany-paneled wall on the right was punctuated with shiny horn-shaped light fixtures, while to the left, a sunken lounge area was filled with Starck-designed furniture. Starck's signature tapered steel legs, and color scheme of white with orange, green, and purple highlights, challenged the bland furniture typically found in hotel lobbies. The guest's promenade along the blue carpet to the reception desk or elevators (both hidden out of sight) functioned as a kind of "runway" raised above the lounge, evoking the experience of a participating in a fashion show.

In the private spaces of the guest rooms, furniture and fittings were also designed by Starck in a similarly idiosyncratic manner. Starck's fastidious attention to detail included handrails shaped like snakes, and the horn shape repeated on door handles, lamps, and vases. The Royalton's interior was marked by playfulness and surrealism, although of the mysterious and suggestive rather than the completely bizarre genre. This became the beginning of many boutique hotels designed by Starck in the 1990s and 2000s, all marked by his distinctive personality and designer cache. Schrager and Starck's success resulted in large, global chain hotels starting to focus on creating boutique experiences that suggest a unique sense of place, personality, or atmosphere.

But creating memorable experiences requires considerable "back-stage" labor. David Brody's research on the hotel as "a realm of coddling where labor seemingly vanishes" raised some pertinent questions about how experiences are staged.[17] He begins by acknowledging that the overwhelming majority of housekeeping staff in the United States are women of color and that housekeeping is low-paid and physically strenuous labor. Brody's research documents the aftermath of a renovation of Chicago's Hyatt Regency in which seemingly superficial changes sparked an industrial dispute. The Hyatt's new rooms included beds with heavier mattresses, white bathrooms with more glass and mirrored surfaces. These details—all designed for an enhanced guest experience—added up to a significant increase in extra cleaning and maintenance for housekeeping.

Designing experiences is intimately tied to marketing and promotion, yet results from a combination of products, systems, and services. As we've seen in previous chapters, the rise of Apple is due to its innovations in these realms, but experience is also essential to its brand strategy. Although well-known for their consistency of visual approach, graphics, packaging, and product design, Apple stores offer consumers a holistic experience. There are over 500 Apple stores around the world, yet their design—and the customer experience—is relatively consistent. Interestingly for a retail store, Apple stores do not have a distinguishable cashier area, suggesting that the brand experience is more important than selling physical products.

Apple stores are characterized by their transparency, particularly large glass doors, windows and glass staircases, and their clean, sparse interiors. This sense of a "dematerialized" architecture and Zen-like ambience resonates with the brand's ethos. In-store graphics match their software interface while the store's minimal use of materials matches their products' clean minimalism. Central to Apple's ideal is a hands-on experience that enables customers to interact with the latest products that are internet connected and loaded with apps. Service strategies, including friendly, approachable technicians ("Geniuses") who try to understand customers' needs and desires, ask questions and show an interest. Products, services, environments, and employee scripts combine to create a holistic customer experience.

In 2016, the Union Square Apple store in San Francisco was redesigned as a model for all future Apple stores. The new features include a "Genius Grove" (complete with trees and plants), "The Plaza," an outdoor space for live concerts and events, "Creative Pros" with specialized knowledge, and "The Forum." Apple's head of retail, Angela Ahrendts, referred to the new stores as "town squares," which aim to be a new type of public gathering places for information exchange and entertainment.[18] But, of course, they are branded experiences, not public spaces. While Apple has adopted the language of city planning—the Avenue, the Plaza, and the Forum—these are temples to Apple that effectively shield their customers from real public spaces of dialogue and protests, poverty and difference.

Immersive entertainment

The quintessential example of a consciously designed experience is Disneyland. Disney's original theme park, opened in California in 1955, offered visitors not simply rides and candy but an immersive world based on Disney's films and cartoons. The park's designers planned a holistic environment in meticulous detail—from the architecture to the lighting fixtures, every form, color, and texture contributed to the visitor experience. Now referred to as "imagineers," Disney's designers create and maintain an escapist world within Disney parks, at once familiar and magical, designed to take visitors out of their everyday lives for a day. Rather than employees, "cast members" in costume provide entertainment in keeping with the theme-based attractions.

Disney's most famous "stage set," Main Street, USA, was based on an idealized, small-town American street. Designed with forced perspective and slightly smaller than regular buildings, its red brick fire station, ice cream parlor, and candy stores evoke intimacy and familiarity. Meticulously detailed signage, ironwork, and fixtures also contribute to the ambience of a turn-of-the-twentieth century town. The eclectic Victorian architecture was never intended as an exactly historical reproduction but designed to elicit emotions from visitors, drawing upon collective memories of idyllic small towns. Importantly, this is not the small-town history of African Americans or indigenous Americans but a sanitized image of the American dream. Safe, clean, and free of wear, Disney's Main Street experience is free from poverty, pollution, and the anxieties of class and race relations.

Disney parks also situate visitors on stage, as both consumers of and producers of the experience, transforming them into actors participating in this other-world. As a designed experience, the Disney park is carefully choreographed escape from everyday life. Storytelling is an essential part of this designed experience, particularly stories and scenes from Disney films. Disney's all-encompassing, theatrical approach to designing the built environment proved influential, with the expansion of Disney parks to Orlando (1971), Tokyo (1983), Paris (1992), Hong Kong (2005), and Shanghai (2016). And Disney's success in designing themed environments spread into other realms, including cafes (such as the Hard Rock Cafes) and flagship stores (such as Niketown).

Casinos are even more carefully calibrated experiences. The wave of themed Las Vegas casinos of the 1990s, for example, engaged ever-more sophisticated design strategies. The massive Venetian casino, with design inspired by Renaissance Italy, offers visitors gondola rides on canals, painted murals, and elaborate Italianate decorations. It also includes theaters, a night club, various dining options, and gaming. The Venetian's sister complex in Macao, China, similarly features imitation fresco paintings on the ceiling, faux marble sculptures, and decorative effects from fiberglass, Styrofoam, and plaster that evoke the delicate tracery and details of Venetian palaces. Such carefully crafted scenography is designed to elicit emotions and immerse visitors in another world.

But the ultimate aim of a casino's sophisticated design is to channel visitors' desires into a single purpose—gambling. Design consultant Bill Friedman's design principles for casinos, published as a book in 2000, documented the now common template—interior planning based on a maze and enticements that "cater to the escapist sensibilities of his clientele."[19]

From creating a cocooned, personal space in which to play a machine so that gamblers become engrossed in gaming, to carefully controlled atmospheric elements, casino designers pay incredible attention to detail. A casino's temperature, light, sounds, and aromas are all carefully designed to elicit reactions from gamers, to entice them to the machines, then immerse them in the gambling zone.

The gaming machines, too, are paradigms of interaction design, designed to evoke intense experiences. Touch screen interfaces respond to gamers' speed, so that the interface will automatically slow or speed up in response to an individual's touch. The increasing move away from inserting coins, notes, or cards into slot machines both divorces the connection to money and speeds up the experience. Sounds are carefully designed to cue particular actions and enhance excitement; animations and visual consistency ensure the interfaces look seductive; and sophisticated ergonomic research into the design of consoles and seating all increase the time people spend gaming. Through onscreen services, gamers can order food and drinks to ensure fewer interruptions to the experience.

As examples of physical immersive environments, Disney parks and casinos are meticulously designed to evoke responses from their visitors. Appealing to people's memories, desires, and sensations is an essential part of such experience design. Designers apply similar principles to the design of virtual worlds, particularly video games, that are also designed with a user's emotional experiences in mind. Grand Theft Auto and Call of Duty, for example, although set in different imaginary worlds, also immerse players within carefully designed sets, sounds, and sensations. Players become characters with interactive encounters, avatars designed to blur the boundaries between the real, physical world and the virtual, digital one.

Tourism

Tourism is based on the production and consumption of experiences. In an attempt to deliver memorable, compelling experiences for tourists, designers and marketers consciously promote and integrate values and meanings into a range of products, services, places, and events. Essentially, tourism aims to generate pleasurable experiences outside of routine work and home life. For designers, increasingly sophisticated research into the means by which to engage a tourist's senses, emotions, and social interactions, as well as understand their motivations, help create such experiences.[20] Part of designing for tourism is trying to create personal engagement via managing service touchpoints, for example, in order to intensify the experience for each individual.

The advent of mass tourism, particularly with the rise of package tours and cruise ships, brought a new focus on designing experiences. By developing a coherent set of services across transportation, accommodation, attractions, and staged cultural performances, mass tourism offers novel experiences within a familiar and predictable framework. Tourist sites such as resorts, museums and galleries, historical and other attractions are carefully designed in order to maintain a coherent aesthetic experience. Increasingly, designing for tourism is becoming an interdisciplinary field that extends across architecture, interiors, products, signage, and information channels such as websites, brochures, and posters in order to create compelling, holistic experiences.

The interactive aspect of design for tourism includes not only physical attractions and facilities, but also intangible elements such as knowledge and information. It requires services and systems to support everything from traditional tourist activities such as sightseeing to more everyday or interactive activities such as dining, attending workshops, or conferences. Tourism often involves coordination on various levels, from public facilities to private businesses and individuals, mediated by state-sponsored and local campaigns, organized groups, and private tour guides. Online accessibility to information and booking services—from Expedia to TripAdvisor—has also changed the way tourist sites coordinate between the virtual and physical realms.

On a smaller scale, digital technologies have changed tourist experiences at particular sites and places. Museums, for example, are embracing digital experiences such as virtual reconstructions using VR headsets, augmented reality via smart phones, gaming scenarios, and narrative videos. This combines information design—to compress complex historical data into understandable information—with various digital tools to create compelling experiences. As one researcher puts it, "new technology offers possibilities for artefacts, historical people, buildings and events to become the characters of a storytelling experience that unfolds in the form of a dialogue between visitors and the museum."[21] In this way, physical artifacts from the past come alive for visitors through virtual stories about their users' lives and context that evoke emotional connections.

A 2017 British Museum exhibition, for example, featured a limestone sculpture carved for a Buddhist temple in India 2000 years ago. Through a link on their smartphone, visitors could activate a projection of a woman dressed in character who explains how and why she commissioned the carving. While her name is unknown, researchers established that she commissioned the carving in the third century and thus can convey information about her culture and beliefs. As an interactive display, the experience did not require the download of an app, but could be controlled through a Wi-Fi link so that visitors' smartphones could access this information about the exhibition. Storytelling and narrative techniques borrowed from video games or films create interactive museum experiences such as this, designed to appeal to a new generation of tourists.

Beyond singular attractions, cities market themselves as tourist hubs for exhibitions, concerts, boutiques, and spectacular architecture. One particular type, "creative cities" promote themselves not just as a passive experience, but as bundles of attractions and activities in which tourists participate and learn via exhibitions, demonstrations, or workshops. In this way, tourist interaction contributes to the local context too, as local creatives learn from tourists, create social networks, or ongoing collaborations. Such destinations are typically marketed for their cultural activities, from café culture, cuisine, fashion, and lifestyle rather than one or two iconic sites. Here, tourists are encouraged to participate in everyday activities with tourists acting in the theater of city life rather than watching it from the safety of an open bus.

Conclusion

Ideally, experience design actively encourages participation, and interaction is central to its success. Pre-created content passively viewed or consumed by visitors does not make for engaging or compelling experiences. As well as the other aspects of design already covered in previous chapters, it is worth stressing that designed experiences involve a narrative aspect—actions unfold over time and are linked via some kind of story. While designers can map these narratives, as in the case of Disney, they should ideally also leave space for visitors' improvisation and creative capacity. In this way, designing experiences draws upon ideas derived from theater, film, and video games as much as traditional design fields. Importantly, experiences need not be simply entertaining, but can be instructive, informative, and inspiring.

Chapter summary

- As well as how things work, designers consider how things make us feel
- Designed products, systems, and services can include or exclude

- Participatory and co-design strategies are essential new approaches for designers
- Designers are starting to acknowledge the limitations of universal solutions
- Creating compelling experiences for all is a fundamentally interdisciplinary pursuit

6

Strategies

If design is a practice dedicated to planning and implementing change, then overlaps with management and governance are inevitable. Recently, designers have staked a claim in shaping organizations, managing projects, mapping future scenarios, and structuring future cities. This extended role for designers has started to shift the popular perception of design. As part of this shift, design is starting to appear into executive boardrooms, high-level government and public service offices, and into non-government and community organizations, to contribute to the foundations of decision-making. At this highest level, designers are not creating tangible things, services or experiences, but proposing strategic solutions to large-scale problems.

Over the past two decades, well-known design consultancies such as IDEO and Frog Design have shifted their focus from designing products to services to offering design solutions on a more strategic level. Popularized as design thinking, design is now being promoted to corporate executives and high-level decision-makers as an alternative to quantitative business analysis. By injecting empathy, user-centered and experimental methods into staid corporate cultures, design promises innovative solutions to complex problems. Along with this new role as management consultants, designers working within government have further broadened design's scope by helping create policies that enable communities and individuals to shape their futures.

Organizational design

In large corporations, design was traditionally seen as an extra feature that occurred once a new product or service had already been conceived. An in-house design team or external consultancy would then shape the product or refine the service before it was delivered to the public. But digital disruption, globalization, and changing consumer expectations have led some executives to adopt a design approach to help solve organizational problems and set managerial agendas. Global companies such as Procter and Gamble, GE, Samsung, and IBM (Case Study 11) have embraced design in a more integrated manner. Rather than bring designers in after the major decisions have been made, designers have been actively engaged in redesigning organizational structures and systems. For organizations, services and interactions are an essential part of their structures, and incorporating design into decision-making offers a more human-centered perspective.

Only in the past decade or so have researchers and practitioners recognized the "invisible" or "silent" design activities already inherent in many organizations.[1] That is, businesses already employ project, engineering, or marketing managers who have always worked in a similar way to designers in the way they conceive and implement change. But design practices such as creating prototypes, service blueprints, and experience scenarios are proving useful in rethinking organizational change. Participatory and co-design techniques for engaging staff and customers, for example, might work not only in developing new products or services, but also in creating a new workplace culture. For designers working in such a capacity, aiding and facilitating collaboration to achieve common goals are as important as visualization and prototyping.

For many corporations today, simply selling more products or services is no longer enough. They are also social organizations that comprise interactions of staff, customers, and investors—various stakeholders who have different views of the corporation's ultimate purpose. At the top, management may be fixated on lowering costs and driving growth. But staff do not necessarily consider optimal efficiency or generating greater profits as their motivation to work. And customers have a different perspective again. Creating a useful product or performing a useful service, making some kind of contribution to society, or having a sense of greater purpose may be the motivating drivers for both staff and customers. A design approach that puts people in the center of organizations can highlight not only customer but also employee engagement, interactions, and experiences.

Traditionally, organizational design is the practice of arranging the best set of people, infrastructure, resources, and services to achieve certain goals. Management consultant Jay R. Galbraith, for example, proposed a method that has had ongoing impact in management circles, "a holistic way of thinking about an organization as consisting of a structure, information decision processes, reward systems, and people."[2] The organization, composed of these elements, should be deliberately configured to achieve the strategic goals of the business. Ideally, management can achieve an optimal arrangement of these components built on principles of efficiency and rational decision-making. But such an approach to management tends to ignore the needs of staff and customers.

As taught in business schools, this approach was characterized by structural rearrangements, altering reporting relationships, and implementing more efficient processes. Driven by large consultancies, business came to be conceived analytically—quantitative data of inputs and outputs are used to make decisions about reorganization. And, rather than the provision of goods, services, or experiences, generating greater profits became the sole aim.[3] The essential management tools comprised a spreadsheet filled with figures and an organizational chart, an abstract map of business units and reporting lines. Fixated on costs and hierarchies, management could easily lose sight of the goods and services the organization produces as well as the needs of their customers and staff.

In contrast, a design approach reconsiders fundamental organizational ideals. Within the organization, this might involve questioning how staff make decisions, manage information, communicate, and collaborate. By including analyses of social interactions and experiences within organizations, we might understand how they affect the production of goods and services. Objective, managerial decision-making is challenged by a design perspective that includes the perspectives of stakeholders within and outside the organization. And, in contrast to a typical analytical approach, which narrows solutions to available data, a design approach to management reframes problems to envisage alternative futures. Embedding such ideas within management has become increasingly popular, particularly in organizations renowned for technological innovation.

An example is Samsung's transformation into a design-led organization. As late as the 1990s, Korean-based Samsung was an electronics company that manufactured cheap copies. The few designers scattered around engineering departments added the final, surface touches to new products. For the most part, these were imitations of Japanese phones and televisions. The cautious management approach focused on using existing technologies, making products cheaper, or processes more efficient. But, in 1996, Chairman Lee Kun-Hee announced a new strategy led by design, to be integrated throughout the organization. From 2000 to 2004, Samsung doubled its design staff and established design centers in London, Los Angeles, San Francisco, Tokyo, and Shanghai. By 2015, Samsung employed over 1,600 designers worldwide.

Samsung's success lay in developing a design-led rather than an engineering-led organization. Beginning in the 2000s, their initial breakthroughs in product design came from combining several digital products into one—a phone, for example, with a camera, music player, and internet access. This led to designing new smartphones and smart TVs. As one Samsung executive explained in 2010, "five years ago, engineers told designers what the products would look like. No more. Now the designers tell the engineers what features they want."⁴ Samsung's designers, along with ethnographers and other researchers, analyzed what their users' needs were and examined their cultural and social contexts in order to better understand their customers.

Going even further, Samsung embedded design within the highest levels of the organization. Samsung's establishment of an in-house design culture extended to a Corporate Design Center devoted to planning strategies for the organization's future. Some of their challenges in redesigning the organization included overcoming resistance to the design-led change, redesigning structures, implementing policies that enabled design, and introducing experimentation into its culture. As testament to their success, Samsung's innovations in the smartphone market meant that it remained the only major smartphone competitor in the wake of the iPhone's dominance. As an organization, Samsung is still redesigning itself from a product-focused to a service-focused one through designing digital platforms for health and transportation services.

Organizational performance, particularly in corporations, is usually quantified in monetary terms. Productivity is linked to incoming revenue or reduction in costs, in implementing efficiencies or streamlining processes that result in greater profits. Yet adopting a customer-centered approach may reveal quite different assumptions about an organization and different ways of conceiving value. Perhaps, rather than incremental change or optimizing workflows in a business-as-usual approach, an organization might create racially different goods, services, or experiences. Working toward a common goal or shared purpose that creates value for customers can lead to a very different type of organization for staff too.

Researcher Sabine Junginger suggests that organizations can potentially reorganize around new product development by envisaging the customer at the center of the organization. She argues that by "embracing the needs and abilities of its customers, the organization can shape itself around them."⁵ That is, unlike Samsung's drive for a design-led culture from within, organizational change may also be achieved by considering transformations from the outside-in. New products or services can actively change a corporation's organizational culture. Here, design's role in transformation differs from top-down management or bottom-up, staff-driven transformation.

Faced with disruption due to automation, changing global conditions, demographics, or increased competition, many organizations are searching for new means to effect change. Their future may lie in alternatives to accepted management practices, particularly ones that require managers to be innovators rather than interpreters of analytics. The idea of management as a design field is one possible direction. As Richard J. Borland Jr argued "managing as designing is the explicit recognition that management is not value free, that it is deeply implicated in shaping and reshaping the social, economic and technological world we live in."[6] Rather than business as usual, design offers organizations the possibility of more radical transformations. To address the complex, systemic problems of organizations, participatory or co-design strategies that can engage various stakeholders can prove valuable.

CASE STUDY 11: IBM

When Thomas Watson Jr became CEO of IBM in 1956, he built a design culture within the organization. Watson's Design Director Eliot Noyes and consultants Paul Rand, Charles and Ray Eames, and architect Eero Sarineen modernized IBM—from its logo to its products, interiors, and architecture—transforming it into the quintessential modern corporation of the 1960s. But, while IBM continued to create innovative technology, design lost ground within the organization. IBM became known as a dull, corporate organization, as opposed to Apple's hip, creative one, at least in the popular imagination.

The famous 1997 defeat of world chess champion Garry Kasparov by IBM's supercomputer, Deep Blue, signaled a new age in which computers had processing powers far beyond humans and hinted at the future possibilities for AI. IBM continued to develop AI, and the latest iteration, Watson, famously defeated human competitors on the quiz show Jeopardy in 2011. Yet, while IBM had technological power, what was missing was connecting it to people who can use it (Figure 14).

FIGURE 14 *Robert "WATSON" from IBM at the annual Mobile World Congress, 2016. Getty Images: Matthias Oesterle/Corbis Images.*

In 2012, CEO Virginia Rometty launched a major design renaissance, with a program to hire over 1,000 designers under the leadership of Phil Gilbert, as well as embed a design thinking program within the company.[7] Now, in addition to over 1,600 designers in forty-four studios around the world, IBM has disseminated design throughout its organization with tens of thousands of its employees completing some kind of design training.

Visualized as "The Loop," the IBM Design Thinking model is founded on building empathy for users, multidisciplinary teams, and continual activity. Based on three steps—"Observe, Reflect, and Make"—the process begins with teams which observe users in action, reflect on that action, then prototype a new product, service, or experience. Situating the user as central in a fundamentally collaborative process was a significant change for a strongly engineering-based organization. And as design thinking was integrated across the company, it started to inform the organization's strategic direction as well as its product development.

Connecting the potential power of AI, cloud computing and robotics to health care, energy, or transportation issues is complex, comprising not only skilled engineering and coding but also designing appropriate user interfaces and experiences. An initiative called "With Watson," for example, offers AI as a service in which Watson can analyze and structure massive quantities of data into usable form. In healthcare, for example, applications include accelerating drug discoveries by trawling data and records for researchers, while diagnostic tools and predictive systems aid healthcare professionals in their care for patients.

Meanwhile, IBM's designers who are designing chatbots, automated programs that can provide services to customers via chat bubbles or voice synthesizers, have encountered a problem: how to design interactions between AI and users? Other IBM projects—from tiny autonomous, robotic cameras that monitor water quality and life in rivers, lakes, and oceans, to complex cryptography systems to protect data, to the potential of quantum computing—also need to be carefully designed for user interaction and aligned to what users need.

Strategic design

In a world characterized by rapid change and uncertainty, strategic design has emerged as a means of implementing a range of new possibilities—rapid iteration of ideas, incorporating end users, and working across knowledge silos—for global corporations and governments. For leaders and managers, strategic design provides an alternative means to see the big picture, consider all aspects of a complex problem, and implement solutions for change and long-term sustainability. Designers engaged with large-scale challenges, such as in healthcare, education, or environmental sustainability, are increasingly dealing with interlinked networks of systems and services, and proposing transformation at a systemic level.

In a corporate context, managers tend to look at hard data in the form of statistics, spreadsheets, or annual reports to make decisions and create long-term strategies. Designers, in contrast, tend to analyze users' needs, desires, and context. CEO of PepsiCo, Indra Nooyi, sought to transform her organization by embedding design in a strategic way. For Nooyi, design went beyond packaging and branding, to "rethink our innovation process and design experiences for our consumers."[8] This included appointing Marco Porcini as chief design officer in 2012 to oversee design-led innovation. Working across the company's numerous products, brands, services, user interactions, and experiences from a design perspective was a significant change for a traditionally conservative organization. Creating a consumer-centered approach on a large scale across a global company required a bold, strategic approach to design.

Strategic thinking refers to thinking about long-term impact, innovation, and new business opportunities within an overall vision to change organizational structures, processes, and systems. Strategic design projects are typically complex and ill-defined, and designers are well-positioned to help formulate strategies for organizations destined for a future clouded with ambiguity and uncertainty.[9] As we have seen, designers within organizations can have an impact in setting goals, initiating new projects, and embedding design thinking. Yet such strategic design need not be limited to large corporations. Increasingly, government and corporate visions need to find some common ground in creating alternative futures for individuals and communities.

Helskini Design Lab, for example, which ran from 2009 to 2013, was a particularly influential practice devoted to addressing complex social problems. It operated out of the Strategic Design Unit of the Finnish Fund for Innovation and worked both within and outside of the Finnish government. The Helsinki Design Lab tackled large-scale systemic issues, such as urban planning, transportation, and education. Part of their role was trying to engage the public in better dialogue and co-creation rather than the traditional government methods of brief consultations and surveys. Also important was their emphasis on inclusive decision-making and implementation of new initiatives, rather than the traditional top-down government approach.

An open-source studio manual, *Recipes for Systemic Change*, explained the Lab's methods and documented a model of their practice. In it, they state: "Our ability to provide for our societies is being challenged by the fact that many of today's problems are structural in nature, with little or no precedent. What do you do when there is no model to copy, no precedent to improve upon?"[10] The publication outlines tools and techniques for conceptualizing and visualizing complex problems, with examples such as how to design a carbon-neutral built environment and how to better deliver services to the elderly. Their education project involved designing a new program for both school dropouts and those who find education not sufficiently challenging, issues that require systemic change in education delivery so as to better incorporate this variety of students.

For long-term sustainability, strategic design offers an approach beyond designing sustainable products or product service systems. As we saw with small-scale examples in Chapter 4, designers have increasingly looked to strategic approaches in order to scale-up sustainable innovations. Living Labs, for example, are one realm for experimentation and testing scenarios that can be easily changed and refined before design solutions are rolled out to the general public. Design's role in social- and community-based innovation on a strategic level involves considering the designer's role as initiator, facilitator, and communicator, in which designers might help shape, envisage, and implement solutions that can empower individuals and communities. Importantly, individuals and communities need to be included within the design process to have any long-term impact.

An example of community-based strategic design is the Cape Town Sustainable Mobility Project, a large-scale project that included a company making wheelchairs, a bicycle association, the Cape Peninsular University of Technology, and Politecnico di Milano. Starting in 2009, the project was later merged into an even larger project, Our Future Cities, aimed at designing more sustainable, equitable, and livable African cities. The Mobility Project's ultimate goal was to design a sustainable product service system to transport the disabled and elderly of Cape Town.[11] Integrating public transport and human-powered options, the project involved consultation with users, transportation officials, local government officials, NGOs, local medical facilities, schools, and media organizations.

Starting with prototypes for a rickshaw-type vehicle, designers worked with the various stakeholders to develop a shared vision that incorporated these new vehicles with the existing public transport infrastructure. For the designers involved, the project included not only developing a product-service system but also the strategies to support its scaling-up, implementation, and ongoing community involvement. To embed the system within the community and ensure its long-term success required sustained engagement with the network of stakeholders over several years. Such an integrated, strategic approach to design creates the best possible conditions for long-term success.

As a response to increased specialization in problem-solving within narrow silos of expertise, strategic design can tackle complex, ill-defined, or interconnected problems in innovative ways. While reproducing solutions on a large scale to create positive change is the ultimate challenge, smaller scale strategies also create impact and benefit people. That is, another way of conceiving strategic design is as a means to consider how individual actions and behaviors combine to affect collective change on a larger scale. For sustainable solutions, reducing, or limiting possibilities, may prove just as transformative as increasing possibilities.

A novel design intervention in this respect is the Light Phone, a credit card-sized phone that only takes and receives calls. Aimed at changing our behavior around the overuse of technology, the designers created the Light Phone as "an invitation to experiences that belong to the user, uniquely, and are free of any dictated experiences related to the product's functional utility."[12] By eliminating functions, the Light Phone is designed "to be used as little as possible." The product seems hardly innovative in itself, yet considered in a particular social context, its effects may provoke a change in user behaviors. In a sense, this minimal phone might provide a different type of freedom—freedom from a smartphone's constant interruptions and distractions that enables users to experience the physical world around them.

One of the underlying premises of strategic design is that it can stimulate innovation, and it is promoted as a catalyst for transformation of an organization, corporation, or government. Innovation is understood as not only the implementation of a new or improved product, service, or system, but also new organizational methods, relations with external stakeholders or systemic diffusion of information or skills. Some of the most successful firms of the twenty-first century have consciously fostered an innovation culture, forming an ecosystem based on multidisciplinary collaboration. Yet for most designers, strategic design operates in a zone far from their traditional skills and expertise. That is, strategic design rarely involves a specific brief to design a new product or service and sketches, prototypes, or service blueprints are less valuable than strategic reports or white papers.

Indeed, if strategic design involves redesigning an organization, or larger scale integration of products, services, or stakeholder inputs, then it seems closer to management than traditional design. And if it includes dealing with various institutions, administrations, and bureaucracies in addressing interconnected systems of people, services, systems, and infrastructure, then the remit of the strategic designer begins to sound more like a CEO or president. For designers who are not trained in organizational management or business administration, understanding structures, policies, and processes and how they interact can seem a long way from their design training and expertise. Such a broad understanding of the ecology of a complex problem with its various facets requires a new type of designer for which there are currently few models or educational opportunities.

Policy

Ideally, governments aim to improve people's lives and have a positive impact on communities. A large part of what governments do is driven by policies aimed at transforming the current situation into a better one. Policies are thus strategic tools that governments use to address large-scale problems or implement reforms. Over the past decade, design's value as a practice dedicated to planning and implementing change has resulted in governments taking more of an interest in design and designers entering into public service organizations (as we saw in Chapter 4). Particularly in Scandinavia and England, design has been recognized as a valuable contribution within governments, with designers involved in shaping policy for complex problems from childhood obesity to affordable housing and effecting change by improving public service provisions.

While governments have used designers as external consultants for a long time, this has typically been for specific, pre-determined products. Particularly in designing visual communications campaigns to promote or inform people about government services, literacy, recycling, or public health, designers have played a role in government provisions. Architecture and urban design have also served as communication tools—from ancient kingdoms to more recent democratically elected governments—the built environment has been used to celebrate a dominant class or shape a certain vision of society. But designers in the twenty-first century have proposed a subtler intervention, with methods and processes to design policies that might better engage citizens in shaping their future.

Denmark's MindLab was one of the first and most successful public sector design labs. It operated between 2002 and 2018 as a cross-Ministry innovation lab within the Danish government. A small group of designers, ethnographers, policy experts worked with public servants to develop new policies that would address complex social and public sector problems. Challenges included reforming the tax experience from a complex mess of incomprehensible forms, procedures, and systems to a more user-friendly experience. Through partnerships, interaction, and mutual learning, MindLab's design methods leaked out into other parts of the government bureaucracy and administrative systems, helping to change its culture. According to Christian Bason, MindLab's director for almost eight years, "In Denmark, a lot of municipalities, local government bodies and state administrations work with user engagement and collaborative innovation methods now. They may not call it co-design, or use other innovation terms, but there's been a major shift in how organisations think and work."[13]

MindLab's impact led to other government and policy innovation labs, centers, and spaces devoted to design in the public sector in various countries and cities around the world. Such spaces are typically housed in a specific physical location that enables different types of relationships and interactions, and aim to be catalysts for innovation. Beyond the traditional siloed thinking of government departments which results in complex and, at times, conflicting regulations and legislations for its citizens, such labs provide a new means for developing policies in a cross-disciplinary manner. Importantly, they aim to be collaborative and inclusive, designing things *with* citizens not simply *for* them, and thus participatory methods are an essential part of their mission.[14]

Founded in 2011, New York City's Public Policy Lab operates along similar principles as MindLab but at a city-wide rather than national scale. Devoted to creating public programs and policies that improve people's lives, the Lab comprises a multidisciplinary team of researchers and designers. Their remit involves working across government agencies to plan, prototype, and implement new public programs and services, and to develop public policies in collaboration with local government agencies. These include programs and social support services for the city's homeless, veterans, and vulnerable student populations. Their work on NYC Well, for example, a one-stop resource for mental health services—crisis intervention, referral, and support—comprises a platform that integrates digital interactions to enable smoother user connections to service providers.

In collaboration with the UK-based Snook design consultancy that has also worked with mental health services and policy, New York's Public Policy Lab has developed a resource identifying what was working and not working in mental health service provision, focusing on user experience across digital channels, text messages, calls, and face-to-face interactions.[15] While elements of the overall public service systems work, they found, within such a complex and fragmented system, touchpoints do not always align for a user. This makes the overall experience difficult and frustrating, and can lead to administrative dead-ends. By mapping user journeys and experiences, such consultancies aim to design better overall systems and experiences for mental health sufferers. Such design projects involve not only examining user interactions with digital services, social media, and wellness apps, for example, but also collaboration with government agencies and other service providers.

Although a relatively new field for designers, Bason suggests three potential contributions of design in policy. First is the mix of design research and visualization that can envisage complex public problems differently, especially through adopting a user-centered perspective; second, tools such as making prototypes, visualizations, scenarios, and user journey maps provide a means for dialogue and collaboration; and third, designers can create the tangible outcomes in the form of graphics, products, services, and systems "that can help give form and shape to policy in practice."[16] That is, designers can convert abstract policies into visible, tangible things. Ideally, government policy labs produce not only these more traditional design outcomes but can also contribute to strategic planning for complex systems and services.

Although innovations in policy have generally been driven from within government or public sector organizations, designers have opened other avenues for large-scale social transformation. Following the steps of design jams and hackathons, the BBC radio program, the Fix, has developed a similar concept for solving large-scale social problems. The program creators work with teams of a dozen young people, including data scientists, ethnographers, economists, and designers, to participate in a design-based workshop. Their aim is to propose alternative approaches to problems such as affordable housing or social isolation. Although the show combines policy planning and design techniques with popular entertainment, its speculative and provocative nature encourages audience participation and engagement.

A more informed public with expectations of transparent decision-making and information, less state intervention, more private providers of public services, demographic changes, and lifestyle expectations have all contributed to a changing policy landscape. For a younger generation who have grown up with different expectations and technologies, part of designing policy includes making government relevant, encouraging voter participation, and active citizenship. But the wholescale shift to interactive digital technologies and tools for informing the public also creates a tension between empowering citizens and "technologies to *create* particular models of citizenship and to endow citizens – whether they like it or not – with particular types of responsibility."[17] Government campaigns aimed at changing behavior, for example, and campaigns designed to shift responsibility from government to citizens often serve to conceal social and economic inequalities.

Finally, it is worth noting the difficulties inherent in designing public policy. One of the biggest problems is the problem of standardized products or services for a diverse population, as governments operate on mass scales rather than for particular individuals or groups. Issues around testing, prototypes, and experimentation are a further challenge for designers working in the public sector as these typically involve a small sample of what may be a very broad population affected by a new policy. Governments also require relatively quick, error-free policies, so participation or co-design involving many citizens over a long period of time is not always possible. Understanding user experiences across a series of touchpoints in complex service environments can be extremely time-consuming and requires significant resources.

Policy implementation is also difficult across a range of government administrations and bureaucracies, resulting in a series of negotiations with various partners. Gaining legitimacy for design labs and design-led solutions in government bureaucracies can also be difficult, as are the problems of dealing with bureaucracies resistant to change or advice from outsiders. And, unlike dealing with corporate leaders who wield power, implementing policies within government can involve dealing with a large number of stakeholders and powerful agencies, each with the power to veto a particular project or idea. Despite these challenges, design for policy is a growing field for designers, particularly with the growing acceptance of design thinking.

Problems and methods

One of the results of design's rise in popularity, particularly in management circles, is the parallel interest in design methods and thinking. Whether or not designers use particular problem-solving methods or exactly which conceptual abilities they bring to a project are ongoing topics of debate, particularly within design circles. Although design thinking has been promoted as a new phenomenon, it is worth briefly reviewing the conceptual basis of design practice over the past fifty years in order to understand if it is as novel as some recent promotors suggest.

In the second half of the twentieth century, professional design splintered into discrete disciplines as earlier titles such as industrial or commercial artist gave way to more specialized ones such as product design engineer or corporate identity designer. This specialization was accompanied by an expansion of design education, particularly within higher education institutes. As part of a widespread anxiety surrounding professions in the 1950s and 1960s, designers began to develop intellectual theories for their practice. An increasing interest in foundational methods and a common language across the increasingly specialized disciplines led to new conceptions of design.

In the 1960s, some designers began to self-consciously relocate design practice away from the conceptualization of things toward more general problem-solving. For design theorists of the 1960s, design was portrayed as a process that could be described and analyzed in abstract terms, free from the particulars of situation and context. Ironically situated against the backdrop of 1960s' social and political unrest, this was a model of problem-solving that was decidedly apolitical. A conspicuous absence of female contributors and a narrow perception of design activities within select developing countries were significant limitations. More recently, design theory has expanded from defining the parameters of the design process to an understanding of this process as a particular mode of thinking and how this might be applied in various contexts.[18]

Attempting to delineate design from other disciplines, some designers and design academics such as Nigel Cross and Kees Dorst focused on design thinking as a distinct form of reasoning, arguing that the design process is founded on "abductive" reasoning and "framing" practices.[19] For increasingly complex design problems in which variables are uncertain, abductive reasoning works from inference to filter possible solutions that are then framed as possible strategies or scenarios. In its extreme manifestations, this approach aims to apply rigorous, scientific processes and avoid judgment, intuition, and creativity. But the fuzzy, poorly defined problems facing designers are rarely the same as those facing scientists.

Designers typically reason by abduction, an inference to the best explanation. In contrast, deductive reasoning is defined by inference as necessarily true (if the premises are true) and inductive reasoning is based on high frequencies or statistical data that have a high probability of being true. Abduction is frequently employed in everyday reasoning—scientists use this mode to predict possible hypotheses and physicians to diagnose the best possible diagnosis based on symptoms. It is, in a sense, a form of educated evaluation. Abductive reasoning uses terms such as probable truth, the most likely possibility or the best possible scenario.

Horst Rittel and Melvin Webber's "Dilemmas in a General Theory of Planning," originally delivered as a 1969 conference paper, explained their influential theory of design's "wicked" (dynamic) versus science's "tame" (static) problems.[20] They begin with a critique of the popular approach to problem-solving among American professionals. Setting goals or objectives, they argue, "requires explication of *desired outcomes*; and then the more recent attempts to build systems of social indicators, which are in effect surrogates for statements of desired conditions." They noted the failure of this approach on a large scale, and argued that political revolts of the 1960s and the growth of consumerism made setting common goals almost impossible. At the same time, Rittel and Webber saw this disintegration of consensus and the new social movements as an opportunity to develop a new conception of design.

Rittel and Webber characterized scientists' problems as "tame," while planning problems are "wicked," or "ill-defined; and they rely upon elusive political judgment for resolution." When faced with "wicked problems," designers cannot follow a consistent, logical process or arrive at definitive solutions. The problem is that wicked problems—unlike say, problems in chemistry or physics—involve people with differing needs, competing agendas, or conflicting personalities. The missing component from simple three-step design thinking processes is understanding the user at the beginning and at the end of process. Initial research is often too time-consuming and costly, as are testing and trials. Even with minimal testing with a limited user sample, the resulting product or service may be better refined. At the other end, post-occupancy evaluations in architecture, surveys, interviews, or observations of new products or services to find out if the solution is really working are rarely included in design thinking models.

In fact, many designed products and services are simply tested in the world. CEOs, politicians, managers, and designers need to work to tight deadlines with limited resources, resulting in less than perfect solutions that are refined on the run. In such a scenario, how do we choose the premises or frame the problem? How do we know this is the best possible solution? Do we design incremental or radical solutions? That is, do we draw upon established models (such as a better phone) versus a completely different idea (a new means of communication). It is worth noting that the world is littered with failed designs. The Museum of Failure in Helsingborg, Sweden, collects innovative failures—from the Apple Newton to Google Glass—products that did not live up to expectations.

CASE STUDY 12: IDEO

Founded in 1991 by David Kelley, Mike Nuttall, and Bill Moggridge, IDEO grew from a Palo Alto-based practice working on consumer products and interaction design to a global consultancy working on systemic and strategic projects. Initially, the company designed high-tech products such as palm pilots, digital cameras, and interactive software. Then they shifted into services and experiences for banking and healthcare, and today IDEO is most closely associated with design thinking. A multidisciplinary practice, IDEO has been influential as a new model of design consultancy focused on user-centered solutions to complex problems.

A campaign created with Bank of America in 2004 illustrates their approach. The bank's brief was to entice more customers to open accounts. IDEO's user-centered process began with ethnographic research into how people actually used bank accounts, including how they saved and spent money. For people struggling financially and living between paychecks, they discovered, establishing a savings plan was not a priority nor even considered a possibility. Insights into these particular customers led IDEO to a new type of banking service.

Their research found a recurring pattern in that mothers, who typically controlled the banking, tended to round up the number in their checkbooks, making addition easier and leaving a little over at the end of the week. Following this practice, IDEO's newly designed service offered customers a savings account that would automatically round up purchases made with cards, then the bank would match this small amount and put the total into a separate savings account. Senior vice president and product developer at the Bank of America Faith Tucker noted "[an] almost unexpected and very emotional effect from this new service."[21] The experience of saving money, no matter the amount, evidently evoked a sense of empowerment and greater financial control for customers (Figure 15).

By analyzing user experiences in this way, IDEO's teams of designers, anthropologists, psychologists, and engineers proposed a "design thinking" as a

FIGURE 15 *Fans compete for prizes at the Common joins Bank of America's Keep the Change Event, Chicago, 2008. Getty Images/Barry Brecheisen/WireImage.*

means to solve a client's briefs. Developing this design thinking process further, IDEO developed a suite of toolkits, such as Method Cards for business innovation, an Educator toolkit, and a Human-Centered Design toolkit. These resources, some of which are freely available online, offer an insight into IDEO's version of design thinking.

Launched in 2010, OpenIDEO functions as an online design thinking platform in which clients submit a brief or challenge, then global users participate to come up with innovative solutions. Most recently, IDEO has launched IDEO.Org, a part of the organization dedicated to improving people's lives in poor and vulnerable communities—healthcare services in India and financial services for poor Americans, for example—IDEO U, a suite of online courses on design thinking, and the Creative Difference, a data-driven, innovation "mastertool" aimed at the corporate market.

Design thinking

Design thinking entered the business world with a series of high profile articles in journals such as *BusinessWeek* and the *Harvard Business Review* over the past decade. Since then, despite the wariness of many designers, design thinking has been promoted as a new business tool to enable empathy, drive innovation, and solve complex problems. Design thinking has spread to MBA programs and educational programs, notably at Stanford University's d. school and Toronto's Rotman Business School. This adoption of the term within business circles has led to both celebration and skepticism among designers, as well as questions about whether design thinking can actually deliver the promised innovations and solutions.

IDEO's Tim Brown claims that his colleague David Kelley first used the term "design thinking" to describe the expanded field that their consultancy operated within. Brown's 2008 article for the *Harvard Business Review* popularized design thinking in the corporate realm as a means to stimulate innovation and increase competitive advantage. In the late twentieth century, argued Brown, design "became an increasingly valuable competitive asset." Rather than the designer as an autonomous creator, he described design thinking as an ethnographic practice in which interdisciplinary teams produce "experiences" comprising "complex combinations of products, services, spaces, and information."[22] Brown oscillates between design thinking as a means to stimulate business innovation and as a means to solve social problems, and this ambivalence continues to characterize IDEO (see Case Study 12).

The design thinking process has been the subject of much speculation and debate. In practice, designers have achieved some common ground in process methods and tools. A common working method is exemplified by the Stanford d. school's five-step design thinking process: empathize, define, ideate, prototype, and test. It also comprises a series of shared characteristics: a collaborative, user-centered, multidisciplinary approach with an iterative process involving rapid prototyping and experimentation. While some designers have argued that such a process has always been inherent in design practice, in a business context, such processes have proven popular in challenging traditional corporate methods and ways to approach complex problems.

Although models of the design thinking process vary—three steps, four steps, five steps—with little agreement over terms, the recurring elements can be summarized as follows:

1   Define and discovery phase, comprising initial research to understand the problem

2   Ideation phase, in which participants generate possibilities

3   Visualization phase, in which the proposed solution is sketched, mapped, or prototyped

Although such models tend to simplify complex processes, they are useful as a means of communication between practitioners operating in different disciplines or knowledge silos. Perhaps it is easiest to understand design's difference when contrasted against similar models of processes in other fields: a business development model, for example, typically involves research, development, and implementation—a sequence that is easy to schedule, budget, and provides clear outcomes. What differentiates the design thinking process is its inherently messy nature, with goals that are not always clear, and steps that are rarely linear, as each phase can return to the first with new insight into the problem.

A design thinking process also differs from a typical scientific method that involves starting from a premise, then formulating a hypothesis, and proposing a repeatable solution. The solution is preferably the only logical consequence that follows from the original premise. But a design project's solution is rarely correct or incorrect—there are merely better or worse solutions (and this is subjective, depending on whose perspective they are viewed from). Scientific reasoning is characterized as objective, whereas design necessarily involves an element of evaluation and judgment.

As practiced, design thinking is often distilled to a process that can be quickly executed. The emphasis on speed and the conceptual processes of designing tend to overshadow the slow, iterative processes usually associated with design. The oversimplification of empathy for users is another limitation, with user workshops or observations completed in a few hours, resulting in superficial understandings. With little time allocated for in-depth research, design thinking can fail to meet its goal of designing a user-centered experience. Empathy and understanding for users typically take a long time, as does building partnerships that enable participation or co-creation.

Design's craft aspects also become marginalized with design thinking. Be they timber or pixels, an intimate knowledge of materials includes knowledge of their possibilities and limits. While design thinking advocates are quick to dismiss the aesthetic aspects of design, this too is an important component of various design outcomes that can be forgotten in rapid ideation, reframing, and implementation. Although some designers in traditional design fields, such as communication or product design, have dismissed design thinking for these reasons, at the very least, it has raised design's profile so that non-designers are paying more attention to design and taking it seriously.

Importantly, design thinking is primarily a North American phenomenon, and not the universally applicable, culturally neutral practice it is assumed to be by its prominent practitioners. As practiced, it is predicated on American forms of innovation, citizenship, and engagement. Perhaps, as it becomes more widely practiced, designers will adapt its methods to alternative cultural contexts. And, as it fades as a popular corporate buzzword, a wider public will continue to recognize design's potential in delivering strategic impacts that can improve the lives of everyone.

Chapter summary

- Design methods can be applied to complex organizational problems
- Designers are increasingly working on strategic levels to address large-scale issues
- Governments are turning to design to aid policy development
- Design is typically understood as a unique approach to problem-solving
- Within the business world, design thinking has shifted the popular perception of design

Conclusion

Trying to grasp the totality of design today—from the simplest graphics and everyday tools to interconnected global systems and services—can seem overwhelming. Yet a basic understanding of design seems essential in order to comprehend the complexity of modern life. And the design processes and activities occurring in the present, as well as those we have inherited from previous generations, are not only affecting our lives today but will also shape our future in fundamental ways. In a sense, design has contributed to both the best and worst aspects of our world, so it deserves both serious consideration and serious rethinking. Ultimately, if we are to improve our condition, design, as a future-oriented discipline, will need to play a significant role.

In the previous six chapters, I have tried to encapsulate the dimensions of contemporary design, from the micro to the macro scale, and to map how these affect our lives on an everyday basis. This short conclusion is both a reflection on some of the larger, ongoing issues for design today, and a reflection on possibilities for design's future. Although these are overlapping, I have divided these reflections into three sections. The first considers design's relationship to larger, planetary processes in terms of the Anthropocene; the second, our modern infatuation with technological solutions; and the final section concludes with some ideas about how we might envisage alternative futures by design.

Design in the Anthropocene

Design's greatest challenge in the twenty-first century is sustainability. Starting in the 1960s, environmental activists drew popular attention to industrialization's and mass consumerism's negative effects. The Club of Rome's 1972 report, *Limits to Growth*, for example, addressed what they termed the "problems of mankind": "accelerating industrialization, rapid population growth, widespread malnutrition, depletion of nonrenewable resources, and a deteriorating environment."[1] Alongside other professionals, designers and design critics began to actively engage with these issues from this time, and the 1970s inaugurated the beginnings of sustainable design.[2] Despite such efforts, and even with public awareness and environmental legislation, the "problems of mankind" not only remained, but also, in many cases, worsened over the last three decades of the twentieth century.

By the first decade of the twenty-first century, the magnitude of these problems, and the growing concern about climate change and its potential effects, led some geologists and earth scientists to coin a new term "the Anthropocene." The Anthropocene describes an era in which human activity is the dominant force in the planet's interacting processes.[3] Greenhouse gases, radioactive isotopes, concrete and plastic particles, ongoing species extinction, deforestation, ocean acidification, and pollution, confirm our profound impact on planetary processes. Central to this concept is a consideration of the planet as an interconnected system—or series of systems—evolving in a dynamic, integrated way. But, compared to the relatively stable eras preceding it, the Anthropocene promises instability and dramatic change.

Importantly, thinking about design in this context entails thinking beyond last century's concept of humanity versus nature. Instead, it evokes interrelated networks of relationships between humans, animals, plants, and larger forces such as the oceans, the seasons, and weather patterns. The Anthropocene also implies thinking in longer time frames: beyond accounting for every minute, maximizing short-term profits or comforts, it requires thinking about the long-term future. Although such scales are hard to connect to seemingly small design decisions, the cumulative effects of using aerosols or plastics, for example, or choosing less materials or none at all, makes a difference.

In the introduction and again in Chapter 4, we encountered bicycle-sharing schemes, a phenomenon that took off in many cities around the world in the mid-2010s. They initially promised a shift from designing, manufacturing, and consuming more material things to designing services and experiences. Such shared transport models seemed like an innovative solution to our over-reliance on cars and fossil fuels, as well as a healthy and sustainable transport option for city dwellers. Rather than rely on individual ownership, sharing service schemes underline the ideas of using resources and energy more efficiently and using material things only when we need them.

In Chinese cities, the bike-sharing industry proved so popular and grew so rapidly that city authorities were forced to introduce regulations to prevent an accumulation of unused bikes littering sidewalks and streets. In 2017, for example, Shanghai city authorities announced a ban on additional share bikes being deployed in the city (Figure 16). As I was finishing this book in September 2018, I traveled to Beijing, where the local government had just announced a plan to limit the number of shared bicycles in the city to less than 2 million. In this example, the design and implementation of a new service system has created additional problems, and may yet turn out to be more unsustainable than individual ownership. This is the type of dilemma faced by contemporary designers.

Yet on a fundamental level, more and more designers today are reconsidering how we produce energy and use resources, where materials come from and where they go, and who is included and excluded from design processes and solutions. Some of the more radical ideas include post-human design in which we might "decenter" humans to acknowledge the impact of a new design on animals, plants, and the planet. Or designers exploring ideas of cohabitation between humans and animals, allowing animals a certain agency in the process, or co-creating new materials with plants (as we saw in the "Materials" section of Chapter 2). A further radical position involves efforts to redesign humans in order to adapt to a changing planet and scarce resources. In the twenty-first century, resilience, flexibility, and adaptation may prove more useful design principles than standardization, form, and function.

FIGURE 16 *Chinese men walk past the abandoned share bicycles stored at a temporary parking lot in Shanghai on August 24, 2017. CHANDAN KHANNA/ AFP/Getty Images.*

Technological fixations

At the beginning of the century, no one had a smartphone, yet today most people consider it an essential tool. And smartphones are only the most visible evidence of the technological changes to our everyday life over the past decade or so. Digital, networked computing has always promised to make our lives more efficient, render the world clearer, and facilitate better solutions. But, despite the ever-increasing speed of calculations, real-time data gathering and processing, and spread of digital devices, ongoing wars, droughts, and famines, species extinction, rising global temperatures, and all manner of social, cultural, and political oppression continue. New technologies have brought us no closer to fixing the "problems of mankind."

Yet the trajectory toward a technological utopia remains an article of faith for many people. An extreme example is embodied in "Death by GPS," a phrase coined by rangers in California's Death Valley, one of the hottest places on earth.[4] Drivers' blind faith in their vehicle's GPS systems leads them onto abandoned trails where they become lost, bogged, or drive over a cliff. Such faith in technological solutions parallels the unquestioning acceptance of digital technology's inevitable takeover of everyday life. For designers, a critical questioning of this technological faith and its foundations address six important issues.

First, the simplistic stories of how new technologies are designed. A tale of a lone genius (usually a white male) toiling away in a garage until a lightbulb moment makes for a dramatic film or documentary, but is inaccurate as a model of how new technologies develop. Innovation is typically incremental, gradual, and grounded in support and research by governments, universities, and corporations. New technologies are stacked onto existing systems—so that the iPhone, for example, required the existing internet and its established protocols. Designing standards, regulations, and policies that enable technological innovations to be implemented on a mass scale (such as the ISO in Chapter 1) is vital yet makes poor cinematic material.

Second, the denial of digital technology's material essence and the accompanying idea that digital tools necessarily use less energy or materials than physical tools are also problematic. The Cloud, the latest metaphor in this dematerialized digital world, sounds like a floating mass of data without any material support structures. But, like all aspects of the internet, it relies on extensive physical infrastructure, from massive air-conditioned data storage centers in remote locations to fiber optic cables and transmission towers. This material infrastructure remains for the most part out of sight and easy to ignore. Consequently, it is difficult to measure how much energy and materials are actually used to create and sustain digital design outcomes.

CONCLUSION

A third vital issue is that data generation, gathering, and analysis are either hidden, opaque, or too complex for non-specialists—including most designers—to understand. Yet many still persist in believing these processes are neutral, objective, and without bias. As we saw in Chapter 1, data is never neutral. Algorithms are designed by people who inevitably shape certain values, enable certain possibilities, or privilege some over othrs. Understanding and overcoming bias, particularly with regards to women, people of color, and people from outside the wealthy West, remain urgent issues. The designers of the next wave of smart tools, devices, and sensors will need to work with data experts in order to understand how their products and services operate.

A fourth consequence of our increased dependence on digital technologies is the power of social media to design our identity. Within only a decade, users of Instagram, Facebook, Tumblr, WhatsApp, LinkedIn, and WeChat have learned to consciously design images of themselves. Our virtual selves are filtered and edited identities in which we can erase blemishes and delete the undesirable. Formerly the realm of professional photographers, now everyone has access to editing, cropping, and filtering photographs, and, like a film director, we also have the ability to piece together a personal narrative over time. Yet the gap between our curated virtual selves and our (imperfect) physical selves is an ongoing cause of concern.

Designing AI applications and interfaces creates a fifth issue for future designers. Currently, most AI applications "learn" pattern recognition through photo sets that train the programs to identify and categorize. Researchers recently found that their AI "amplified predictable gender biases found in the photos – going so far as to categorize a man standing next to a stove as a woman."[5] Such amplification of existing stereotypes confirms the need for a greater understanding of these technologies before they are deployed into our designed services and experiences. And, as with other digital technologies discussed above, AI-driven experiences rely on hidden material infrastructure and labor. To put it another way, what are the resources and energy that we really expend every time we ask Alexa the weather forecast?

Robots comprise the sixth aspect of a seemingly unstoppable technological determinism. Haunted by the specter of replacement by a machine, workers across a wide range of industries are beginning to feel vulnerable, if not disposable. Yet the idea of robots doing our jobs ascribes agency to machines, not to managers and CEOs actively investing in labor-saving technologies designed to replace workers (and thereby increase profits). Not surprisingly, the threat of robots is used as both a management tool to drive down wages and a warning to low-paid workers. As our current app interfaces give users the idea that a ride simply materializes, or food appears at the door as if conjured by magic, will future self-driving cars, automated factories, and personal assistant robots also hide their labor, energy, and resource expenditures behind a seamless interface? What role will designers play?

Design futures

Ultimately, the technological ideals we have inherited are embedded within a particular way of living and thinking that designers today are challenging from a number of perspectives. As the idea of technology as universal, neutral, and unbiased no longer holds, designers face a different set of ethical decisions. And new technologies represent only one aspect of our designed future. Given the expansion of design's remit—into experiences, strategies, policies, and governance—designers are also engaged in problems for which technology offers little help. Social, political, and cultural problems require social, political, and cultural solutions.

Design is a fundamentally future-oriented discipline, and part of its role is projecting possibilities for action. Changing the Accelerating Modernization of the twentieth century requires an alternative narrative or vision, perhaps an entirely new way of conceiving design. Design theorist Tony Fry frames design practice around the concepts of "futuring" and "defuturing" to describe design directed toward a more or less sustainable future state. Fry suggests that changing our concept of design might slow the rate of defuturing and redirect us "towards more sustainable modes of planetary habitation."[6] This force of redirection, he argues, involves a new political and ethical foundation for designers. Rather than simply design for profit, disruption, or distraction, we require more compelling, inspirational, and inclusive visions.

Similarly, design theorist Stuart Walker's "Journey in Design" describes the contrasting journeys of two explorers of North America, John Franklin and Samuel Hearne.[7] Franklin's technologically sophisticated and overloaded 1845 expedition ended in disaster while Hearne, seventy-five years earlier, "travelled light, and looked to the indigenous people for guidance and instruction," adopting a more sustainable approach. Continuing this allegory, Walker suggests that design is founded on exploration, and that to "be a designer is to be on uncertain ground." Design's professionalization has resulted in limiting preconceptions, argues Walker, but improvisation and the integration of indigenous design ideas could provide future directions toward more suitably sustainable practices.

While Walker's allegory has merit, his explorers are both complicit with colonialism. The indigenous people who proved guidance and instruction were—presumably—not on uncertain ground. As we saw in previous chapters, acknowledging indigenous design is not simply adapting some skills or acknowledging a presence, but involves a deeper understanding of indigenous knowledge and alternative world-views. This includes alternative concepts of social life, and human relationships to the environment and the cosmos. On the one hand, this is an essential part of decolonizing design. On the other, it indicates that our rush for innovation often neglects existing indigenous systems, services, and products, which may need updating or changing yet still work perfectly well.

A further problem in considering such complex issues is how to construct a design language that is genuinely global and universally understood. Discussions of globalization often assume some common purpose, concepts, subject matter, or language. But this also inevitably includes an erasure of difference and particularity. The past two hundred and fifty years of design discourse was dominated overwhelmingly by designers, critics, and writers from Europe and America, necessarily marginalizing other perspectives. This needs correction. So too does the accompanying notion that design is a supporting partner to technological development that occurs primarily in advanced capitalist economies. Considering design from an indigenous perspective or within alternative cultures or economies can provide alternative future possibilities.

In the twenty-first century, the continuing threat of extinction to cultures, languages, and ways of life as well as to non-human species and habitats has resulted in a characterization of profound changes driven by global processes out of control. But, such changes are generally implemented *by design*, and, intentional or not, these processes are driven by humans. A recent reaction to this is the rise of design activism, in which design processes are not characterized as a service by professional designers for clients but as proactive interventions or "disruptive" and self-consciously political activities.[8] At their best, such projects force us to imagine various futures—utopian or dystopian—and help us re-envisage our concepts of technology, science, or social relations.

Another important contribution for informing future design activities is research. While much of this is in the form of user interviews or ethnographic studies, there is also a broader interest among designers in incorporating different approaches and perspectives. Following this, design education's future shape and connection to practice, government, and business may be equally important in determining design's future roles.[9] The rise of higher research degrees in design, while relatively new, suggests that the next generation of designers may be highly educated professionals with expertise across various fields. This may signal a shift from Silicon Valley's "move fast and break things" mantra to a more considered "move slow and fix things" approach.

Future designers and critics must engage with design's ethical, cultural, economic, and political dimensions if they are to make a genuinely sustainable contribution. The preceding chapters focused not only on the outcomes of design and the skills or processes that produced them, but also on the planning, reflection, and thinking that precedes that action. That is, design is understood as the imagination to envisage something better as well as the skills to implement it. This will require future designers to develop not only research skills alongside visualization skills, but also skills in dialogue, negotiation, and collaboration to truly improve the state of our complex world.

Notes

Introduction

1. Berry's popular quote has circulated around social media for the past decade. The original source is an online article, John D. Berry, "Tables of Contents," *Creative Pro*, March 21, 2007: https://creativepro.com/dot-font-tables-of-contents/ [accessed August 1, 2018].
2. Gary Huswit's 2007 documentary *Helvetica* is a good introduction to Helvetica's spread and reception, as is the chapter by Kerry William Purcell in Grace Lees-Maffei, ed., *Iconic Designs: 50 Stories about 50 Things*, London: Bloomsbury, 2014, pp. 80–83. For a comprehensive account, see Victor Malsy and Lars Müller, eds., *Helvetica Forever: The Story of a Typeface*, Baden: Lars Müller Publishing, 2009.
3. Kalashnikov told his remarkable story—from his childhood in a remote peasant village to an obsessive (yet entirely self-taught) weapon designer—in Mikhail Kalashnikov (with Elena Joy), *The Gun that Changed the World*, trans. by Andrew Brown, Cambridge and Malden, MA: Polity Press, 2006; Michael Hodges, *AK47: The Story of the People's Gun*, London: Sceptre, 2007, traced the weapon's spread across various global conflict zones from the 1950s to 2004; and C. J. Chivers's book, *The Gun*, New York: Simon and Schuster, 2010, is a comprehensive analysis of the AK-47 in the broader contexts of both earlier weapons manufacturing and the 1940s Soviet Union. The reference to Kalashnikov's final letter is from Luke Harding's article in "Kalashnikov Inventor Haunted by Unbearable Pain of Dead Millions," *The Guardian*, January 14, 2014: https://www.theguardian.com/world/2014/jan/13/kalashnikov-weapon-inventor-spiritual-pain-dead-millions [accessed August 1, 2018].
4. Louis Sullivan, "The Tall Building Artistically Considered," *Lippincott's Magazine*, March 1896, p. 408. Sullivan's original, poetic text read: "Whether it be the sweeping eagle in his flight, or the open apple-blossom, the toiling workhorse, the blithe swan, the branching oak, the winding stream at its base, the drifting clouds, over all the coursing sun, **form ever follows function**, and this is the law."
5. Glenn Adamson, *The Invention of Craft*, London and New York: Bloomsbury, 2013, argues that craft is "a modern invention" (p. xiii), defined during the industrial revolution as a "counterpoint to industry" (p. xiv).
6. Two non-specialist introductions to engineering are: Natasha McCarthy, *Engineering: A Beginner's Guide*, Oxford: Oneworld Publications, 2009; and David Bockley, *Engineering: A Very Short Introduction*, Oxford: Oxford University Press, 2012. Henry Petroski's essays on engineering, collected

in his many books, are not only readable but also enlightening in their focus on the role of design in engineering. See, Henry Petroski, *To Engineer Is Human: The Role of Failure in Successful Design*, New York: St Martin's Press, 1985; Henry Petroski, *The Evolution of Useful Things*, New York: Alfred A. Knopf, 1992; and Henry Petroski, *Invention by Design: How Engineers Get from Thought to Thing*, Cambridge, MA: Harvard University Press, 1997.

7   In Geoffrey Matstutis, *Architecture: An Introduction*, London: Lawrence King, 2010, he notes that architectural practice is ancient, yet "as settlements became more complex it became necessary to plan developments rather than rely upon an ad hoc accretion of structures. This increasingly complexity called for design—the ability to envision a future and mediate the building process to achieve that future" (p. 6).

8   See, for example, Colin Combe, *Introduction to Management*, Oxford: Oxford University Press, 2014, p. 5.

9   United Nations, Department of Economic and Social Affairs, Population Division, "World Population Prospects: The 2017 Revision, custom data acquired via UN website," 2017: http://www.un.org/en/development/desa/population/ [accessed August 1, 2018].

10 Pew Research Institute, "Mobile Fact Sheet," January 12, 2017: http://www.pewinternet.org/fact-sheet/mobile/ [accessed August 1, 2018].

11 World Bank, *World Development Report 2016: Digital Dividends*, Washington, DC: World Bank, 2016: http://www.worldbank.org/ [accessed August 1, 2018].

12 I have borrowed this ordering from Richard Buchanan's "Four Orders of Design," first proposed in Richard Buchanan, "Wicked Problems in Design Thinking," *Design Issues*, 8:2, 1992, pp. 5–21.

Chapter 1

1   Alvin Toffler, *Future Shock*, London: Pan Books, 1970. On pp. 318–323 Toffler discusses the psychological effects of overstimulation brought about by accelerating change and information processing.

2   I owe this idea to Alexander R. Galloway, see his "Theory of Media," January 15, 2018: http://cultureandcommunication.org/galloway/a-theory-of-media [accessed April 8, 2018].

3   Peter Drucker, "The Coming of the New Organization," *Harvard Business Review*, January 1988.

4   Beatrice Wardle, "The Crystal Goblet, or Printing Should Be Invisible," in Michael Bierut, Jessica Helfand, Steven Heller, and Rick Poynor, eds., *Looking Closer 3: Classic Writings on Graphic Design*, New York: Allworth Press, 1999, pp. 56–59.

5   Jorge Frascara, *Communication Design: Principles, Methods, and Practice*, New York: Allworth Press, 2004, p. 67.

6   Kevin Larson and Rosalind Picard, "The Aesthetics of Reading," Human-Computer Interaction Consortium, February 2005, Colorado. Conference paper: https://affect.media.mit.edu/pdfs/05.larson-picard.pdf [accessed April 8, 2018].

7   Marshall McLuhan, *The Gutenberg Galaxy: The Making of Typographic Man*, London: Routledge and Kegan Paul, 1962.

8   W. A. Dwiggins, "New Kind of Printing Calls for New Design," *Boston Evening Transcript*, August 29, 1922.

9   Jan Tschichold, *The New Typography: A Handbook for Modern Designers*, trans. by Ruari McLean, Berkeley and Los Angeles: University of California Press, 1998.

10 Paul Rand, "Good Design Is Good Will," *Design, Form, Chaos*, New Haven and London: Yale University Press, 1993, p. 41.

11 Ken Garland, "First Things First," 1964: http://www.manifestoproject.it/ken-garland/ [accessed April 8, 2018].

12 See "Graphical symbols for use on equipment": https://www.iso.org/obp/ui#iso:pub:PUB400008:en. The latest version, ISO 7000 / IEC 60417 "Graphical symbols for use on equipment" was published by the International Electrotechnical Commission, a non-profit, non-government standards organization. The line within a broken circle—technically referred to as the "standby signal"—is IEC 60417-5009.

13 Standards Organizations recommend comprehension levels for successful pictograms. The International Standards Organization, for example, recommends at least 67 percent comprehension, the American National Standards Institute, 85 percent.

14 Steven Heller, *The Swastika: Symbol beyond Redemption*, New York: Allworth Press, 2000, p. 15.

15 The story of NTT DoCoMo's innovative "i-mode" service, that integrated web-based interactions, is retold in an interview with Takeshi Natsuno in Bill Moggridge, *Designing Interactions*, Cambridge, MA: MIT Press, 2017, pp. 393–410.

16 Vyvyan Evans, "The Power of Emoji," CNN, July 18, 2017: "Emojis have become, without a doubt, a design classic. But how effective are they as a communication tool? Over 6 billion emojis are sent on a daily basis, with over 90 percent of the world's online community making regular use of them. Emojis may be one of Japan's greatest-ever exports." (http://edition.cnn.com/style/article/emoji-digital-language/index.html). Instagram statistic from Engineering Instagram, May 1, 2015: https://engineering.instagram.com/emojineering-part-1-machine-learning-for-emoji-trendsmachine-learning-for-emoji-trends-7f5f9cb979ad.

17 Kazuko Koike, Naoto Fukasawa, Kenya Hara, and Takashi Sugimoto, *MUJI*, New York: Rizzoli, 2010, p. 120. Hara also discusses emptiness in Hara, *Designing Design*, Baden: Lars Müller Publishers, 2007, pp. 241–243.

18 Edward Tufte, *Envisioning Information*, Cheshire, CT: Graphics Press, 1990, p. 34.

19 Otto Neurath in Christopher Burke, Eric Kindel, and Sue Walker, eds., *Isotype: Design and Contexts, 1925–1971*, London: Hyphen Press, 2013, p. 85.

20 They are borrowing this concept from philosopher Donna Haraway. See Catherine D'Ignazio and Lauren F. Klein, "Feminist Data Visualization," Workshop on Visualization for the Digital Humanities (VIS4DH), Baltimore, 2016: http://vis4dh.dbvis.de/papers/2016/Feminist%20Data%20Visualization.pdf [accessed August 1, 2018].

21 See GEL: http://www.bbc.co.uk/gel/guidelines/how-to-design-infographics [accessed February 18, 2018].

22 William Morris, "A Note by William Morris on His Aims in Founding the Kelmscott Press," 1898, in Clive Ashwin, ed., *History of Graphic Design and Communication: A Sourcebook*, London: Pembridge Press, 1983, p. 238.

Chapter 2

1 Judy Attfield, *Wild Things: The Material Culture of Everyday Life*, Oxford and New York: Berg, 2000, p. 11.

2 Although his system was based on standardization, Model T Fords were in fact available in a range of colors. Henry Ford (with Samuel Crowther), *My Life and Work: Expanded and Annotated Edition*, Boca Raton, FL: CRC Press, 2013, p. 54.

3 Brooks Stevens Associates brochure, 1953, quoted in John Heskett, "The Desire for the New: The Context of Brooks Stevens's Career," in Glenn Adamson, ed., *Industrial Strength Design: How Brook Stevens Shaped Your World*, Cambridge, MA and London: MIT Press, 2003, p. 4.

4 Harold Van Doren, "Introduction," in *Industrial Design: A Practical Guide*, New York and London: McGraw-Hill Book Company, 1940, p. xvii. In the revised, second edition, Van Doren adds, "Stripped of hocus-pocus, the goal of design is sales—at a profit." Harold Van Doren, *Industrial Design: A Practical Guide to Product Design and Development*, New York and London: McGraw-Hill Book Company, 1954, p. xvii.

5 Le Corbusier, *The Decorative Art of Today*, trans. by James I. Dunnett, London: The Architectural Press, 1987, p. 72.

6 Roland Barthes, *Mythologies*, trans. by Annette Lavers, London: Paladin, 1973, p. 95.

7 I. Kopytoff, "The Cultural Biography of Things: Commoditization as Process," in A. Appadurai, ed., *The Social Life of Things: Commodities in Cultural Perspective*, Cambridge: Cambridge University Press, 1986. Daniel Miller, *Material Culture and Mass Consumption*, Oxford and Cambridge, MA: Blackwell, 1987.

8 See the 2009 documentary, *Handmade Nation*, and Faythe Levine and Cortney Heimerl, *Handmade Nation: The Rise of DIY, Art, Craft and Design*, New York: Princeton Architectural Press, 2008.

9 Sarah R. Davies, "Characterizing Hacking: Mundane Engagement in US Hacker and Makerspaces," *Science, Technology and Human Values*, 43:2, 2018, p. 177.

NOTES

10 In Chinese classical literature such as *The Water Margin* (also known as *Outlaws of the Marsh*), "Shanzhai" refers to the home of the bandits, and "more often than not, these outlaws are the Chinese equivalent of Robin Hood." Fan Yang, "From Bandit Cell Phones to Branding the Nation: Three Moments of *Shanzhai*," Fan Yang, ed., *Faked in China*, Indianapolis: Indiana University Press, 2015, p. 64. See Yang, "From Bandit Cell Phones to Branding the Nation," pp. 64–90, and Andrew Chubb, "China's Shanzhai Culture: 'Grabism' and the Politics of Hybridity," *Journal of Contemporary China*, 24:92, 2015, pp. 260–279.

11 Chubb, "China's Shanzhai Culture," p. 267.

12 Braungart and McDonough are drawing on biomimicry, the principle of "innovation by nature" in which we treat nature as "Model, Measure and Mentor." See also Janine Benyus, *Biomimicry: Innovation Inspired by Nature*, New York: Harper Perennial, 2002, p. 2.

13 Neri Oxman, "Templating Design for Biology," *Architectural Design*, 85:5, 2015, pp. 100–107.

14 The Guardian: https://www.theguardian.com/books/2017/apr/27/screen-fatigue-sees-uk-ebook-sales-plunge-17-as-readers-return-to-print.

15 Paul Polak, "Design for the Other Ninety Percent," in Cynthia E. Smith, ed., *Design for the Other 90%*, New York: Cooper-Hewitt National Design Museum, 2007, p. 19.

16 Penny Sparke, *As Long As It's Pink: The Sexual Politics of Taste*, London: Pandora, 1995.

17 See: https://motherboard.vice.com/en_us/article/mgb3yn/technology-isnt-designed-to-fit-women

See: https://www.smithsonianmag.com/innovation/the-worlds-first-true-artificial-heart-now-beats-inside-a-75-year-old-patient-180948280/?no-ist

18 Patricia A. Moore, "Experiencing Universal Design," in Wolfgang F. E. Preiser and Elaine Ostroff, eds., *Universal Design Handbook*, New York: McGraw-Hill, 2001, pp. 2.1–2.12.

Chapter 3

1 For an excellent overview, see Paul Atkinson, *Computer*, London: Reaktion Books, 2010.

2 Donald Norman, *The Design of Everyday Things*, Revised and Expanded Edition, New York: Basic Books, 2013, p. 11.

3 See this 2017 report in the *New York Times*: https://www.nytimes.com/2017/09/07/health/epipen-fda-malfunction.html. This followed 2016 reports and Congress hearings that the company was effectively using its monopoly position with the device to gouge consumers and the government. A two-pack rose to $600—for a drug that costs $10, it made a return to old fashioned syringes a reality. For the return to syringes, see the PBS report: https://www.pbs.org/newshour/health/as-epipen-prices-skyrocket-consumers-and-emts-resort-to-syringes-for-life-threatening-

allergies. Around this time, a hacker group posted a DIY video on how to make your own home-made version, the EpiPencil.

4   Bruno Latour (Jim Johnson), "Mixing Humans with Non-Humans: Sociology of a Door-Closer," *Social Problems*, 35, 1988, pp. 298–310.
5   I owe these ideas to anthropologist Lucy Suchman, see *Human-Machine Reconfigurations: Plans and Situated Actions*, London and Cambridge, MA: Cambridge University Press, 2006, esp. p. 10–17.
6   Juhani Pallasmaa, *The Eyes of the Skin: Architecture and the Senses*, Chichester: Wiley and Sons, 2012, p. 62.
7   Norman, *The Design of Everyday Things*, p. 133.
8   Wendy Ju and Larry Leifer, "The Design of Implicit Interactions: Making Interactive Systems Less Obnoxious," *Design Issues*, 24:3, 2008, p. 81.
9   See Charles Hannon, "Gender and Status in Voice User Interface," *Interactions*, 32:3, 2016, pp. 34–37.
10 See Brenda Laurel, *Computers as Theater*, Second Edition, Upper Saddle River, NJ: Addison-Wesley, 2013.
11 Steven Johnson, *Interface Culture: How New Technology Transforms the Way We Create and Communicate*, New York: Basic Books, 1997, p. 14.
12 For an excellent overview, see Larissa Hjorth, Jean Burgess, and Ingrid Richardson, eds., *Studying Mobile Media: Cultural Technologies, Mobile Communication and the iPhone*, London: Routledge, 2012.
13 See Mike Kuniavsky, *Smart Things: Ubiquitous Computing User Experience Design*, Burlington, MA: Elsevier, 2010, pp. 57–68 for a detailed analysis of the smart fridge.
14 See the Dunne and Raby website: http://www.dunneandraby.co.uk/content/projects/10/0.
15 Cathy O'Neil, *Weapons of Math Destruction: How Big Data Increased Inequality and Threatens Democracy*, London: Penguin Books, 2017.
16 See Shaowen Bardzell, "Feminist HCI: Taking Stock and Outlining an Agenda for Design," CHI 2010: CHI for All, Atlanta, GA, 2010.

Chapter 4

1   US Department of Labor statistics on employment—data from 2016, see: https://www.bls.gov/emp/tables/employment-by-major-industry-sector.htm. It is important to note that the production of things has only declined in some economies while offshore production has seen manufacturing increase in countries such as China, India, and Mexico.
2   George Ritzer, *McDonaldization: The Reader*, Third Edition, Thousand Oaks, CA: Pine Forge Press, 2010, p. 16.
3   A good introduction to systems thinking in general is Donella H. Meadows, *Thinking in Systems: A Primer*, White River Junction, VT: Chelsea Green Publishing, 2008.

NOTES

4   Braungart and McDonough are drawing on biomimicry, the principle of "innovation by nature" in which we treat nature as "Model, Measure and Mentor."

5   Drawing upon existing ideas of Scandinavian design excellence, as well as progressive welfare state ideals of equality and democracy, IKEA's Swedish design connection and emphasis on Swedishness was ultimately connected to their global expansion in the 1980s. See Sara Kristofferson, *Design by IKEA: A Cultural History*, London: Bloomsbury, 2014, pp. 51–77, chapter 3, "Swedish Stories and Design."

6   G. Lynn Shostack, "How to Design a Service," *European Journal of Marketing*, 16:1, 1982, p. 55. See also G. Lynn Shostack, "Designing Services That Deliver," *Harvard Business Review*, 62:1, 1984, pp. 133–139.

7   Mary Jo Bitner, "Servicescapes: The Impact of Physical Surroundings on Customers and Employees," *Journal of Marketing*, 56, April 1992, p. 57.

8   Lucy Kimbell, "The Turn to Service Design," in Guy Julier and Liz Moor, eds., *Design and Creativity: Policy, Management and Practice*, Oxford and New York: Berg, 2009, p. 158.

9   See Eva-Maria Kirchberger and Bruce S. Tether, "Specialist Service Design Consulting: The End of the Beginning, or the Beginning of the End?" in Daniela Sangiorgi and Alison Prendiville, eds., *Designing for Service: Key Issues and New Directions*, London and New York: Bloomsbury, 2017, pp. 65–77.

10 See: *The Guardian*, 2017: https://www.theguardian.com/sustainable-business/2017/jun/19/shebah-is-the-women-only-ride-sharing-service-we-should-not-need-but-do [accessed June 16, 2018].

11 In a San Francisco study, without a ride-sharing option, 39 percent of ride-share passengers would have taken a taxi, 33 percent public transport, and a further 10 percent walked or biked. Speed and convenience were cited as the most important reasons for choosing ridesharing. See Lisa Rayle, Susan Shaheen, Nelson Chan, Danielle Dai, and Robert Cervero, "App-Based, On-Demand Ride Services: Comparing Taxi and Ridesourcing Trips and User Characteristics in San Francisco," *University of California Transportation Center Working Paper*, November 2014, online at US Department of Transportation: https://www.its.dot.gov/itspac/dec2014/ridesourcingwhitepaper_nov2014.pdf [accessed June 16, 2018].

12 Mareike Glöss, Moira McGregor, and Barry Brown, "Designing for Labour: Uber and the On-Demand Mobile Workforce," CHI'16, ACM conference paper, San Jose, CA, 2016.

13 British Design Council, "Design Methods for Developing Services": https://www.designcouncil.org.uk/sites/default/files/asset/document/Design%20methods%20for%20developing%20services.pdf

14 Gerard Briscoe and Catherine Mulligan, "Digital Innovation: The Hackathon Phenomenon," Creativeworks Working Paper No.6, London, 2014: http://www.creativeworkslondon.org.uk/wp-content/uploads/2013/11/Digital-Innovation-The-Hackathon-Phenomenon1.pdf [accessed July 18, 2018].

15 Lilly Irani, "Hackathons and the Making of Entrepreneurial Citizenship," *Science, Technology and Human Values*, 40:5, 2015, p. 801.
16 Ezio Manzini and François Jégou, *Sustainable Everyday: Scenarios of Urban Life*, Milan: Edizioni Ambiente, 2003, pp. 70–71.
17 Singanapalli Balaram, "Invisible Design: The Alternative Approaches," *Thinking Design*, New Delhi: Sage, 2011, pp. 193–205.
18 See http://www.rita.com.mx/. For more detailed analysis of this as a service design case study, see Carla Cipolla and Javier Reynoso, "Service Design as Sensemaking Activity: Insights from Low-Income Communities in Latin America," in Daniela Sangiorgi and Alison Prendiville, eds., *Designing for Service: Key Issues and New Directions*, London: Bloomsbury, 2017, pp. 147–161.
19 Ezio Manzini, *Design, When Everyone Designs: An Introduction to Design for Social Innovation*, Cambridge, MA: MIT Press, 2015, p. 31.
20 Further information on the service design processes of ACCESS NYC are here: Part 1: https://civicservicedesign.com/case-study-access-nyc-part-1-5ccdf1c4a520 and Part 2: https://civicservicedesign.com/case-study-access-nyc-part-2-f86130ebdead

Chapter 5

1 Raymond Loewy, *Never Leave Well Enough Alone*, Baltimore: The John Hopkins University Press, 1951.
2 Alternative keyboard arrangements include Dvorak and Colemak.
3 Paul Hekkert and Hendrik N. J. Schifferstein, "Introducing Product Experience," in *Product Experience*, Oxford: Elsevier, 2011, p. 4. See also Paul Hekkert and Pieter Desmet, "Framework of Product Experience," *International Journal of Design*, 1:1, 2007, pp. 57–66.
4 Roberto Verganti, *Overcrowded: Designing Meaningful Products in a World Awash with Ideas*, Cambridge, MA and London: MIT Press, 2016, p. 56. For a fuller account, see Roberto Verganti, "Designing Breakthrough Products," *Harvard Business Review*, October 2011, pp. 115–120.
5 As well as a reference to Thomas More's visionary novel, UTOPIA is an acronym for Utbildning, Teknik Och Produkt, Arbetskvalitetsperspektiv, or Training, Technology, and Product in Work Quality Perspective. See Yngve Sundblad, "UTOPIA: Participatory Design from Scandinavia to the World," in John Impagliazzo, Per Lundin, Benkt Wangler, eds., 3rd History of Nordic Computing (HiNC), October 2010, Stockholm, Sweden. Springer, *IFIP Advances in Information and Communication Technology*, AICT-350, pp. 176–186, 2011, History of Nordic Computing 3.
6 Useful overviews of the development of these practices are Elizabeth B. –N. Sanders's "From User-Centered to Participatory Design Approaches," in Jorge Frascara, ed., *Design and the Social Sciences: Making Connections*,

London and New York: Taylor and Francis, 2002, pp. 1–8; and Sanders E., and Stappers, P. J., "Co-Creation and the New Landscapes of Design," *CoDesign: International Journal of CoCreation in Design and the Arts*, 4:1, 2008, pp. 5–18.

7   See Eric Von Hippel, *Democratizing Innovation*, Cambridge, MA and London: MIT Press, 2005, "Chapter 2: Development of Products by Lead Users," pp. 19–31.

8   See the AIGA website: https://eyeondesign.aiga.org/against-crowdsourcing-logo-design-an-open-letter-from-aiga-to-the-tokyo-olympic-committee/

9   See: www.maketools.com [accessed September 12, 2018].

10 The European Network of Living Labs, for example, founded in 2006: https://enoll.org/.

11 The Center for Humane Technology is a non-profit organization founded by former Silicon Valley technology specialists, now dedicated to designing humane technology: http://humanetech.com/.

12 Rosemary Garland-Thomson, "Misfits: A Feminist Materialist Disability Concept," *Hypatia: A Journal of Feminist Philosophy*, 26:3, 2011, p. 594. I am borrowing this idea from Elizabeth Guffey, *Designing Disability: Symbols, Space, and Society*, London and New York: Bloomsbury, 2018.

13 Maria Rogal and Raúl Sanchez, "Co-Designing for Development," in Rachel Beth Egenhoefer, ed., *Routledge Handbook of Sustainable Design*, Abingdon, UK: Routledge, 2017, p. 257.

14 See, for example, the Decolonizing Design Collective website: http://www.decolonisingdesign.com

15 Guffey, *Designing Disability*, p. 146.

16 B. Joseph Pine and James H. Gilmore, "Welcome to the Experience Economy," *Harvard Business Review*, July–August 1998, pp. 98. See also B. Joseph Pine and James H. Gilmore, *The Experience Economy*, updated edition, Boston: Harvard Business Review Press, 2011.

17 David Brody, *Housekeeping by Design: Hotels and Labor*, Chicago: The University of Chicago Press, 2016, p. 23.

18 See Angela Ahrendts's presentation, "The Future of Apple Stores—Apple Keynote 2017," YouTube: https://www.youtube.com/watch?v=NKgHi3v8A1U

19 Natasha Dow Schull, *Addiction by Design: Machine Gambling in Las Vegas*, New York: Princeton University Press, 2012, p. 40. I owe these ideas to Schull, particularly chapter 2 of her book, "Interior Design for Interior States: Architecture, Ambience and Affect," pp. 35–51.

20 See, for example, Iis P. Tussyadiah, "Toward a Theoretical Foundation for Experience Design in Tourism," *Journal of Travel Research*, 53:5, 2014, pp. 543–564.

21 Federica Dal Falco and Stavros Vassos, "Museum Experience Design: A Modern Storytelling Methodology," *The Design Journal*, Supplement 1, Design for Next: Proceedings of the 12th European Academy of Design Conference, Sapienza University of Rome, April 12–14, 2017, p. S3979.

Chapter 6

1. Peter Gorb and Angela Dumas, "Silent Design," *Design Studies*, 8:3, 1987, pp. 150–156.
2. Jay R. Galbraith, *Designing Organizations: An Executive Guide to Strategy, Structure and Process*, Third Edition, San Francisco: Jossey-Bass, 2014, p. 17.
3. Richard Buchanan, "Design on New Ground: The Turn to Action, Services and Management," in Sabine Junginger and Jürgen Faust, eds., *Designing Business and Management*, London and New York: Bloomsbury, 2016, p. 19.
4. Tony Mitchell, *Samsung Electronics and the Struggle for Leadership of the Electronics Industry*, Singapore: John Wiley and Sons (Asia), 2010, p. 157.
5. Sabine Junginger, "Product Development as a Vehicle for Organizational Change," *Design Issues*, 24:1, 2008, p. 33.
6. Richard J. Borland Jr, "On Managing as Designing," in Rachel Cooper, Sabine Junginger, and Thomas Lockwood, eds., *Handbook of Design Management*, London: Bloomsbury, 2013, p. 537. See also Richard J. Borland Jr and Fred Collopy, eds., *Managing as Designing*, Stanford: Stanford University Press, 2004.
7. Steve Lohr, "IBM's Design-Centered Strategy to Set Free the Squares," *New York Times*, November 14, 2015: https://www.nytimes.com/2015/11/15/business/ibms-design-centered-strategy-to-set-free-the-squares.html [accessed August 22, 2018]; Brian O'Keefe, "How IBM Is Training Its Workforce to Think like Designers," *Fortune*, December 22, 2017: http://fortune.com/2017/12/22/ibm-design-thinking/ [accessed August 22, 2018].
8. Adi Ignatius, "How Indra Nooyi Turned Design Thinking into Strategy: An Interview with PepsiCo's CEO," *Harvard Business Review*, September 2015: https://hbr.org/2015/09/how-indra-nooyi-turned-design-thinking-into-strategy [accessed August 20, 2018].
9. Keiran Duck, "Executing Strategy: What Designers Can Teach Project Managers," *Design Management Review*, 23:2, 2012, pp. 28–36.
10. Bryan Boyer, Justin W. Cook and Marco Steinberg, *Recipes for Systemic Change*, Helskini: Helskini Design Lab, 2011, p. 20: http://www.helsinkidesignlab.org/peoplepods/themes/hdl/downloads/In_Studio-Recipes_for_Systemic_Change.pdf
11. More detailed description of this project is in Fabrizio Ceschin, *Sustainable Product-Service Systems: Between Strategic Design and Transition Design*, Heidelberg: Springer, 2014, pp. 84–99.
12. John Bruce, "Design Strategies for Impact," in Rachel Beth Egenhoefer, ed., *Routledge Handbook of Sustainable Design*, 2017, p. 35.
13. Jennifer Guay, "How Denmark Lost Its MindLab: The Inside Story," Apolitical Blog, June 5, 2018: https://apolitical.co/solution_article/how-denmark-lost-its-mindlab-the-inside-story/ [accessed August 19, 2018].
14. On the early history of MindLab, see, Helle Vibeke Carstensen and Christian Bason, "Powering Collaborative Policy Innovation: Can Innovation Labs Help?" *The Innovation Journal: The Public Sector Innovation Journal*, 17:1, 2012, pp. 2–26.

15 See Sarah Drummond, "Positive Patterns for Designing Mental Health Services," Pixel Patterns blog, October 5, 2017: https://pixelpioneers.co/blog/2017/designing-for-mental-health-with-service-patterns [accessed August 17, 2018]; and Sarah Drummond, "Designing Mental Health Services with Public Policy Lab and Snook," Medium, March 27, 2018: https://medium.com/@sarahdrummond/designing-mental-health-services-with-public-policy-lab-and-snook-58f4516fb375 [accessed August 17, 2018].
16 Christian Bason, *Design for Policy*, London: Routledge, 2014, pp. 4–5.
17 Liz Moor, "Designing the State," in Guy Julier and Liz Moor, eds., *Design and Creativity: Policy, Management and Practice*, Oxford and New York: Berg, 2009, p. 30.
18 See the two-part overview of design thinking by Lucy Kimbell, "Rethinking Design Thinking," *Design and Culture*, 3:3, 2011, pp. 285–306 and 4:2, 2012, pp. 129–148.
19 Kees Dorst, "The Core of 'Design Thinking' and Its Application," *Design Studies*, 32:6, 2011, pp. 521–532.
20 Horst Rittel and Melvin Webber, "Dilemmas in a General Theory of Planning," *Policy Sciences*, 4, 1973, pp. 155–169. See also Buchanan, "Wicked Problems in Design Thinking," pp. 5–21.
21 Quoted in Eli Woolery, *Design Thinking Handbook*: https://www.designbetter.co/design-thinking [accessed August 17, 2018].
22 Tim Brown with Barry Katz, *Change by Design: How Design Thinking Transforms Organizations and Inspires Innovation*, New York: Harper Business, 2009, p. 6. Tim Brown, "Design Thinking," *Harvard Business Review*, June 2008, pp. 1–9.

Conclusion

1 Donella H. Meadows, Dennis L. Meadows, Jørgen Randers, and William W. Behrens III, *The Limits to Growth: A Report for the Club of Rome's Project on The Predicament of Mankind*, New York: Universe Books, 1972, p. 21. Rachel Carson's *Silent Spring*, Boston: Houghton Mifflin, 1962, brought pesticide use and environmental pollution into public consciousness, while the *Whole Earth Catalog*, published from 1968, promoted tools and practices for more environmentally sensitive individual lifestyles. This coincided with the foundation of public advocacy organizations such as Friends of the Earth (1969) and Greenpeace (1970). In design, systems thinking on a global scale were represented by Richard Buckminster Fuller's *Operating Manual for Spaceship Earth*, Carbondale, IL: Southern Illinois University Press, 1969.
2 Two useful summaries of early ecological design are Pauline Madge, "Design, Ecology, Technology: A Historiographical Review," *Journal of Design History*, 6:3, 1993, pp. 149–166; and Pauline Madge, "Ecological Design: A New Critique," *Design Issues*, 13:2, 1997, pp. 44–54.
3 A good overview is Jeremy Davies, *The Birth of the Anthropocene*, Berkeley: University of California Press, 2016. In one of the first published articles on

the Anthropocene, Paul J. Crutzen and Eugene F. Stoermer, proposed the later part of the eighteenth century, coinciding with James Watt's invention of the steam engine, as the beginning of the Anthropocene. See Paul J. Crutzen and Eugene F. Stoermer, "The 'Anthropocene'," *IGBP Newsletter*, 41, 2000, pp. 16–18; and Simon L. Lewis and Mark A. Maslin, "Defining the Anthropocene," *Nature*, 519, March 12, 2015, pp. 171–180.

4   Greg Milner, "Death by GPS: Are Satnavs Changing Our Brains?" *The Guardian*, June 25, 2016: https://www.theguardian.com/technology/2016/jun/25/gps-horror-stories-driving-satnav-greg-milner.

5   Jieyu Zhao, Tianlu Wang, Mark Yatskar, Vicente Ordonez, and Kai-Wei Chang, "Men Also Like Shopping: Reducing Gender Bias Amplification Using Corpus-level Constraints," Copenhagen: Proceedings of the 2017 Conference on Empirical Methods in Natural Language Processing, September 2017.

6   Tony Fry, *Design Futuring: Sustainability, Ethics and New Practice*, Oxford and New York: Berg, 2009, p. 6.

7   Stuart Walker, "Design Process and Sustainable Development," *Sustainable by Design: Explorations in Theory and Practice*, London and Sterling, VA: Earthscan, 2012. See also the excellent recent anthology, Stuart Walker and Jacques Giard, eds., *The Handbook of Design for Sustainability*, London: Bloomsbury, 2013.

8   See, for example, Alistair Fuad-Luke, *Design Activism: Beautiful Strangeness*, London and Sterling, VA: Earthscan, 2009; Carl DiSalvo, *Adversarial Design*, Cambridge, MA and London: The MIT Press, 2012; and an overview by Thomas Markussen, "The Disruptive Aesthetics of Design Activism: Enacting Design between Art and Politics," *Design Issues*, 29:1, 2013. Tony Fry argues that designers, and all "agents of change," need to "learn how to move design out of its economic function and into a political frame," Tony Fry, *Design as Politics*, Oxford and New York: Berg, 2011, p. viii.

9   Networks such as the Designers Accord, 2007–2012, a "global coalition of designer, educators, and business leaders working together to create positive environmental and social impact": http://www.designersaccord.org/, and DESIS (Design for Social Innovation and Sustainability), a network of design labs, based in design schools and universities, actively promoting and supporting sustainable change: http://www.desis-network.org/.

Annotated guide to further reading

Most people go straight for an internet search engine when seeking information about a given topic. Unfortunately, searches related to design typically lead to "inspirational" websites devoted to images of lifestyle accessories, fashionable clothing, designer interiors, new gadgets, or funky fonts. Such sites contain many compelling images but rarely contain any thoughtful analysis. Below are recommended starting points for further information about design, both online and in print.

Websites

Design Observer: https://designobserver.com. Founded in 2003, *Design Observer* is an online repository of original articles, podcasts, and external links. Affiliated with the American Institute of Graphic Arts (AIGA), *Design Observer* is particularly rich in visual communication-related sources.

Core 77: http://www.core77.com. Founded in 1995, *Core 77* focuses on product- and industrial design-related issues, and includes original articles, discussion forums, and professional services.

Dezeen: https://www.dezeen.com/. Founded in 2006, Dezeen focuses on architecture, interiors, and product design. A curated selection, it includes articles, forums, and professional services.

Interaction Design Foundation: https://www.interaction-design.org/. Founded in 2002, the Foundation has an educational focus and a large, open source reference library that includes an essential resource for interaction design, *The Encyclopedia of Human-Computer Interaction*.

DESIS (Design for Social Innovation and Sustainability): https://www.desisnetwork.org/. Founded as a global network in 2009, DESIS links universities, institutions, design labs, and individuals on a platform that contains resources related to social innovation and design.

Podcasts

Debbie Millman's "Design Matters" is an essential collection of over 200 interviews with leading designers and critics. https://www.designmattersmedia.com/designmatters

The Radiotopia team behind "99 Percent Invisible" focuses on "the unnoticed architecture and design that shape our world" and has produced over 300 episodes since 2010. https://99percentinvisible.org/

Jessica Hefland and Michael Bierut's "The Design of Business, The Business of Design" comprises interviews with designers across various disciplines. https://soundcloud.com/designofbusiness-businessofdesign

Introduction

John Heskett, *Design: A Very Short Introduction*, Oxford and New York: Oxford University Press, 2005 (the second edition of Heskett's 2002 *Toothpicks and Logos: Design and Everyday Life*).

Concise yet holistic, Heskett's influential introduction encapsulates the wave of globalization and digital technologies that re-oriented design practice, thinking, and methods in the 1990s. It includes a brief history of design, and short chapters on function and human values, objects, communications, environments, identities, systems, contexts, and futures. Heskett's frequent examples and insight into design's role within businesses and policy make this a readable and relevant introduction.

Mike Press and Rachel Cooper, *The Design Experience: The Role of Design and Designers in the Twenty-First Century*, Aldershot and Burlington: Ashgate, 2003.

Drawing upon sociology and cultural studies, Press and Cooper's concise introduction covers topics such as design research, processes, communication, professional issues, and future possibilities. Their focus on designers as "cultural intermediaries that provide goods and services with forms, packagings and presentations", and design as an economic activity make this another good introduction.

Hazel Clark and David Brody, eds., *Design Studies: A Reader*, Oxford and New York: Berg, 2009.

Clark and Brody's anthology comprises a diverse sample of perspectives and authors. Their collection of extracts from classic texts and short articles focuses on topics such as design history, design thinking, design theory, identity and consumption, labor and industrialization, globalization, and includes case studies of iconic objects.

Chapter 1

Malcolm Barnard, *Graphic Design as Communication*, Abingdon, UK: Routledge, 2005.

Jorge Frascara, *Communication Design: Principles, Methods, and Practice*, New York: Allworth Press, 2004.

These two accessible introductions have slightly different aims. Barnard's is more theoretical and focuses on communication design's relationship to society and culture. Frascara's is aimed at practitioners, and includes an overview of the field, as well as the methods involved in production and practice. Also from Allworth Press, the numerous *Looking Closer* anthologies are useful resources for anyone interested in communication design.

Johanna Drucker, *Graphesis: Visual Forms of Knowledge Production*, Cambridge, MA: Harvard University Press, 2014.

Drucker's *Graphesis* is an excellent overview of contemporary visual culture and essential reading for anyone interested in communication design. Her main argument is that because so much contemporary information and knowledge is image-based, we need to develop a more sophisticated and critical understanding of how to read and understand visual forms.

Edward R. Tufte, *Envisioning Information*, Cheshire, CT: Graphics Press, 1990.

Tufte's classic book on information design remains a landmark publication and good starting point. Filled with visual examples and detailed analysis, it is an essential resource for anyone interested in understanding charts, diagrams, maps, and other visual means of communicating information.

Chapter 2

Prasad Boradkar, *Designing Things: A Critical Introduction to the Culture of Objects*, Oxford and New York: Berg, 2010.

A comprehensive overview of new ways of understanding how things are designed, used, and perceived. Boradkar examines the relationship between design and objects as an interactive one, operating within larger systems of manufacture, consumption, and culture.

Leslie Atzmon and Prasad Boradkar, eds., *Encountering Things: Design and Theories of Things*, London: Bloomsbury, 2017.

A wide-ranging collection of essays that survey the renewed interest in things as "the central, inevitable media of design." Key themes include how things operate in dynamic networks, the power that things have in affecting our lives, and the role of design in shaping things that shape us.

Gary Huswit, director, *Objectified*, documentary film, 2009.

A follow-up to Huswit's 2007 documentary on *Helvetica*, this documentary on contemporary product design is based on interviews with practitioners, including Dieter Rams, Jonathan Ive, and Hella Jongerius, critics such as Alice Rawsthorn, and curators Paola Antonelli and Andrew Blauvelt.

Elizabeth Shove, Matthew Watson, Martin Hand, and Jack Ingram, *The Design of Everyday Life*, Oxford and New York: Berg, 2007.

A good introduction to design and material culture from a sociological perspective. Based on a series of interviews with consumers, the authors consider how people interact with everyday products—from plastic containers to digital cameras—as well as how professionals and non-professionals design and modify things.

Chapter 3

Bill Moggridge, *Designing Interactions*, London and Cambridge, MA: MIT Press, 2007.
Although some of the technology discussed is dated, Moggridge's collection of interviews and contextual essays on interaction design remains a classic. The focus on interaction with new technologies, from the Star GUI to later multimedia devices, adaptive technologies, services, and software, provides a wealth of relevant ideas from practitioners.

Donald Norman, *The Design of Everyday Things*, revised and expanded edition, New York: Basic Books, 2013.
Updated and expanded, Norman's popular introduction to human-product interaction argues for well-designed products in "a world filled with frustration, with objects that cannot be understood, devices that lead to error." Focusing on badly designed in addition to well-designed products, Norman's is a good introduction to the complexity of our relationship with everyday things.

Lucy Suchman, *Human-Machine Reconfigurations: Plans and Situated Actions*, second edition, Cambridge: Cambridge University Press, 2007.
First published in 1987, Suchman's introduction to human–computer interaction was updated and expanded twenty years later. Suchman combines a social scientific approach with theories from computer science, artificial intelligence, and interface design. Her compelling ideas about how we have blended machines into our lives highlight the gaps between the limitations of machines and human expectations and behaviors.

Brenda Laurel, *Computers as Theatre*, second edition, Reading, MA: Addison-Wesley Professional 2014.
Another updated classic, Laurel's introduction to human–computer interaction is essential reading for anyone interested in interface design. Her analysis of the dramatic structure and the emotional experience we have with digital technologies touches on not only computers, but also online games, social networks, smart devices, and augmented reality.

Chapter 4

Anna Meroni and Daniela Sangiorgi, eds., *Design for Services*, Farnham: Gower, 2011.
Comprising a diverse range of sources and case studies, Meroni and Sangiorgi's anthology is an ideal introduction to service design. Moving beyond the design of tangible things, they argue for a new framework that takes into account not only services' immaterial dimension and ephemeral nature, but also customers, staff, and the varying situations that affect service design.

Rachel Cooper, Sabine Junginger and Thomas Lockwood, eds., *Handbook of Design Management*, London: Bloomsbury, 2013.
This collection of essays focuses on design's more recently expanded role within organizations and its relationship to strategy and leadership, that is, the role of design in management and the role of management in design. It provides a

good overview of the practices, methods, and theories at the intersection of business, organizational, and management approaches to design.

Ezio Manzini, *Design, When Everyone Designs: An Introduction to Design for Social Innovation*, Cambridge, MA and London: MIT Press, 2015.

Manzini's inspiring introduction to social design is founded on the idea that in a world of rapid and profound change, individuals and collectives must develop their design capabilities. The basis of this, he argues, rests on better understanding and enabling collaborative practices and refocusing design efforts from an emphasis on problem solving to a practice founded on values.

Chapter 5

Paul Hekkert and Hendrik N. J. Shifferstein, *Product Experience*, Oxford: Elsevier, 2011.

A comprehensive collection of articles on product design, use, interaction, and experience. Although academic in tone, Hekkert and Shifferstein's anthology provides a good survey of psychology-based design research that delves deeply into our emotional, sensual, and cognitive interactions with, and experience of, designed products.

Patrick Newbery and Kevin Farnham, *Experience Design: A Framework for Integrating Brand, Experience, and Value*, Hoboken, NJ: John Wiley and Sons, 2013.

Written from a practitioner perspective, this is an accessible introduction to experience design. Newbery and Farnham's framework, predominantly a business-focused one, emphasizes how design can generate more value from products and services through creating better holistic customer experiences.

Anna Klingmann, *Brandscapes: Architecture in the Experience Economy*, Cambridge, MA: MIT Press, 2007.

Klingmann's overview is a good introduction to how physical buildings and urban spaces can be charged with meaning and emotional values—and how they are consciously designed as experiences. From Disney to Las Vegas, she considers the impact of designed places in the creation of identity of corporate, cultural, and social identities.

Chapter 6

Richard J. Borland Jr, and Fred Collopy, eds., *Managing as Designing*, Stanford: Stanford University Press, 2004.

This now-classic collection of presentations originated in a workshop devoted to design's relationship to management. From a variety of perspectives, these essays comprise a solid introduction to design for management and a call for design-oriented problem-solving applied in business contexts. Within this is a call for management education and practice to adopt some design vocabulary in order to change decision making processes and organizational cultures.

Christian Bason, ed., *Design for Policy*, Farnham, UK: Gower, 2014.

Bason's edited collection features articles from government strategists, public service managers, design experts, and academics on policy and design in government and community organizations. Case studies offer a global perspective of policy design in practice at various levels and highlight some of the current difficulties of implementing change in complex contexts such as government.

Nigel Cross, *Design Thinking*, Oxford and London: Berg, 2011.

Cross's introduction to design thinking comprises both theoretical sections and short case studies. In this influential account of design thinking, Cross argues that design "is a key part of what makes us human." With a focus on problem-solving processes and abductive reasoning, this is a clear and accessible starting point for anyone interested in delving deeper into design theory and thinking.

Tim Brown with Barry Katz, *Change by Design: How Design Thinking Transforms Organizations and Inspires Innovation*, New York: Harper Business, 2009.

Aimed predominantly at a business audience, Brown's accessible and popular introduction is another good starting point for further reading on design thinking. Brown's design thinking process operates within interdisciplinary teams that produce "experiences" comprising "complex combinations of products, services, spaces, and information." Using case studies from IDEO, Brown proposes design thinking as a key to both business innovation and solving social problems.

Conclusion

Tony Fry, *Design Futuring: Sustainability, Ethics and New Practice*, Oxford and New York: Berg, 2009.

Fry's classic text is framed around the question, "How can a future be secured by design?" His notion of design futuring involves slowing the rate of destructive change and redirecting design practices toward more sustainable models. At once an ethical and political challenge, Fry's book also contains numerous case studies as examples of how these aims might be achieved.

Select bibliography

Adamson, Glenn, *The Invention of Craft*, London and New York: Bloomsbury, 2013.
Appadurai, Arjun, ed., *The Social Life of Things: Commodities in Cultural Perspective*, Cambridge: Cambridge University Press, 1986.
Atzmon, Leslie, and Prasad Boradkar, eds., *Encountering Things: Design and Theories of Things*, London: Bloomsbury, 2017.
Balaram, Singanapalli, *Thinking Design*, New Delhi: Sage, 2011.
Barnard, Malcolm, *Graphic Design as Communication*, Abingdon, UK: Routledge, 2005.
Bason, Christian, *Design for Policy*, Abingdon, UK: Routledge, 2014.
Bason, Christian, *Leading Public Sector Innovation: Co-Creating for a Better Society*, Bristol: Policy Press, 2010.
Black, Alison, Paul Luna, Ole Lund, Sue Walker, eds., *Information Design: Research and Practice*, Abingdon, UK: Routledge, 2017.
Boradkar, Prasad, *Designing Things: A Critical Introduction to the Culture of Objects*, Oxford and New York: Berg, 2010.
Borland, Richard J., and Fred Collopy, eds., *Managing as Designing*, Stanford: Stanford University Press, 2004.
Brown, Tim, with Barry Katz, *Change by Design: How Design Thinking Transforms Organizations and Inspires Innovation*, New York: Harper Business, 2009.
Buchanan, Richard, "Wicked Problems in Design Thinking," *Design Issues*, 8:2, 1992, pp. 5–21.
Buurman, Gerhard, ed., *Total Interaction: Theory and Practice of a New Paradigm for the Design Disciplines*, Basel: Birkhäuser, 2005.
Cooper, Rachel, Sabine Junginger, and Thomas Lockwood, eds., *Handbook of Design Management*, London: Bloomsbury, 2013.
Cross, Nigel, *Design Thinking*, Oxford and London: Berg, 2011.
Dorst, Kees, *Understanding Design*, second edition, Corte Madera, CA: Gingko Press, 2006.
Drucker, Johanna, *Graphesis: Visual Forms of Knowledge Production*, Cambridge, MA: Harvard University Press, 2014.
Drucker, Peter, "The Coming of the New Organization," *Harvard Business Review*, January 1988.
Egenhoefer, Rachel Beth, *Routledge Handbook of Sustainable Design*, Abingdon, UK: Routledge, 2017.
Forty, Adrian, *Objects of Desire: Design and Society since 1750*, London: Thames and Hudson, 1986.
Frascara, Jorge, *Communication Design: Principles, Methods, and Practice*, New York: Allworth Press, 2004.

Fry, Tony, *Design Futuring: Sustainability, Ethics and New Practice*, Oxford and New York: Berg, 2009.

Gorb, Peter, ed., *Design Management*, London: Architecture, Design and Technology Press, 1990.

Hekkert, Paul, and Hendrik N. J. Shifferstein, *Product Experience*, Oxford: Elsevier, 2011.

Hekkert, Paul, and Pieter Desmet, "Framework of Product Experience," *International Journal of Design*, 1:1, 2007, pp.57–66.

Helfand, Jessica, *Design: The Invention of Desire*, New Haven and London: Yale University Press, 2016.

Huppatz, D. J., *Design: Critical and Primary Sources*, 4 volumes, London: Bloomsbury, 2016.

Jacobson, Robert E., ed., *Information Design*, Cambridge, MA: MIT Press, 1999.

Julier, Guy, *The Culture of Design*, second edition, London: Sage Publications, 2008.

Julier, Guy, and Liz Moor, eds., *Design and Creativity: Policy, Management and Practice*, Oxford and New York: Berg, 2009.

Junginger, Sabine, and Jürgen Faust, eds., *Designing Business and Management*, London: Bloomsbury, 2016.

Kimbell, Lucy, "Rethinking Design Thinking: Part 1," *Design and Culture*, 3:3, 2011, pp. 285–306.

Kimbell, Lucy, "Rethinking Design Thinking: Part 2," *Design and Culture*, 4:2, 2012, pp. 129–148.

Kirkham, Pat, ed., *The Gendered Object*, Manchester and New York: Manchester University Press, 1996.

Krippendorf, Klaus, *The Semantic Turn: A New Foundation for Design*, New York: Taylor & Francis CRC, 2006.

Lankow, Jason, Josh Ritchie, and Ross Crooks, *Infographics: The Power of Visual Storytelling*, Hoboken, NJ: John Wiley and Sons, 2012.

Latour, Bruno, *Reassembling the Social: An Introduction to Actor-Network-Theory*, Oxford: Oxford University Press, 2007.

Laurel, Brenda, *Computers as Theatre*, second edition, Reading, MA: Addison-Wesley Professional, 2014.

Lawson, Bryan, *How Designers Think: The Design Process Demystified*, Oxford and Burlington, MA: Architectural Press, 2006.

Lees-Maffei, Grace, ed., *Iconic Designs: 50 Stories about 50 Things*, London: Bloomsbury, 2014.

Lees-Maffei, Grace, and Rebecca Houze, eds., *The Design History Reader*, Oxford and New York: Berg, 2010.

Manovich, Lev, *Software Takes Command*, London: Bloomsbury, 2013.

Manovich, Lev, *The Language of New Media*, Cambridge, MA: MIT Press, 2001.

Manzini, Ezio, *Design, When Everyone Designs: An Introduction to Design for Social Innovation*, Cambridge, MA: MIT Press, 2015.

Martin, Roger, *The Design of Business: Why Design Thinking Is the Next Competitive Advantage*, Cambridge, MA: Harvard University Press, 2009.

McDonough, William, and Michael Braungart, *Cradle to Cradle: Remaking the Way We Make Things*, New York: North Point Press, 2002.

Meroni, Anna, and Daniela Sangiorgi, eds., *Design for Services*, Farnham: Gower, 2011.

Miller, Daniel, *Material Culture and Mass Consumption*, Oxford and Cambridge, MA: Blackwell, 1987.
Moggridge, Bill, ed., *Designing Interactions*, Cambridge, MA: MIT Press, 2007.
Mollerup, Per, *Data Design: Visualising Quantities, Locations, Connections*, London: Bloomsbury, 2015.
Nelson, H. G., and Erik Stolterman, *The Design Way: Intentional Change in an Unpredictable World*, second edition, Cambridge, MA: The MIT Press, 2012.
Norman, Donald, *The Design of Everyday Things*, revised and expanded edition, New York: Basic Books, 2013.
Papanek, Victor, *Design for the Real World: Human Ecology and Social Change*, second edition, Chicago: Academy Chicago Publishers, 1984.
Petroski, Henry, *To Engineer Is Human: The Role of Failure in Successful Design*, New York: St Martin's Press, 1985.
Robertson, Frances, *Print Culture: From Steam Press to Ebook*, Abington and New York: Routledge, 2013.
Sangiorgi, Daniela, and Alison Prendiville, eds., *Designing for Service: Key Issues and New Directions*, London: Bloomsbury, 2017.
Shove, Elizabeth, Matthew Watson, Martin Hand, and Jack Ingram, *The Design of Everyday Life*, Oxford and New York: Berg, 2007.
Sparke, Penny, *As Long As It's Pink: The Sexual Politics of Taste*, London: Pandora, 1995.
Suchman, Lucy, *Human-Machine Reconfigurations: Plans and Situated Actions*, second edition, Cambridge: Cambridge University Press, 2007.
Thackera, John, *In the Bubble: Designing in a Complex World*, Cambridge, MA: MIT Press, 2005.
Verbeek, Peter-Paul, *What Things Do: Philosophical Reflections on Technology, Agency, and Design*, trans. by Robert P. Crease, Philadelphia: Pennsylvania State University Press, 2005.
Verganti, Roberto, *Overcrowded: Designing Meaningful Products in a World Awash with Ideas*, Cambridge, MA: MIT Press, 2016.
Von Hippel, Eric, *Democratizing Innovation*, Cambridge, MA and London: MIT Press, 2005.
Walker, Stuart, *Sustainable by Design: Explorations in Theory and Practice*, London and Sterling, VA: Earthscan, 2012.
Walker, Stuart, and Jacques Giard, eds., *The Handbook of Design for Sustainability*, London: Bloomsbury, 2013.

Index

ABC 20
Accelerated Modernization 9, 10, 146
accessibility 44, 81, 96, 108, 111, 117
ADA (Americans with Disabilities Act) 109, 111
Adidas 50
advertisements 2, 7, 17, 20, 23, 24, 27, 28, 42, 90, 109
advertising 7, 8, 12, 17, 19, 20, 22, 23, 26, 35, 39, 42, 54, 68, 70, 102, 106
affordances 60–3
AI (Artificial Intelligence) 10, 32, 57, 125–6, 145
AIGA (American Institute of Graphic Arts) 19, 105
Airbnb 27, 35, 69, 88
Alexa 66, 75, 145
algorithms 68, 76, 91, 100, 102, 106, 107, 145
American Airlines 2
Anthropocene 9, 15, 141–2
anthropological methods 60, 87
anthropologists 42, 57, 60, 99, 135
anthropology 65, 84
Apple 5, 20, 22, 23, 25, 41, 42, 44, 49, 59, 66, 70–2, 81, 113–14, 125, 135
   iPad 65
   iPhone 5, 25, 41, 42, 65, 70–2, 81, 124, 144
   iPod 70, 81
   iTunes 79, 81
application (app) 1, 8, 11, 17, 21, 24, 32, 66–8, 71–5, 82, 85, 88–91, 96, 114, 117, 131, 145
architect 2, 4, 6, 7, 9, 39, 46, 50, 51, 63, 81, 82, 108, 125
architecture 6, 7, 31, 103, 114, 115, 117, 118, 125, 130, 134

Arntz, Georg 30
Attfield, Judy 37
automation 38, 40, 57, 64, 69, 76, 124, 126, 146
automobile 7, 9, 10, 21, 37, 38, 39, 40, 42, 50, 57, 58, 60, 66, 90, 91, 142, 146

Balaram, Singanapalli 93–4
Barthes, Roland 41–2
Bason, Christian 130–1
Bauhaus 9, 19
Bayer, Herbert 19
BBC 34, 132
Beck, Henry C. 32
Berry, John D. 1
Bic 54
bicycle 9, 11, 12, 38, 60, 81, 88, 128, 143
biomaterials 37, 40, 50, 51, 83
blueprints 1, 85, 91, 122, 129
Borland, Richard J. 124–5
brand 26–8, 28, 33, 35, 42, 49, 61, 67, 69, 70, 85, 114
branding 7, 8, 12, 19, 26, 27, 33, 35, 42, 54, 87, 127
Braungart, Michael 50, 51, 82
Breuer, Marcel 6
Brody, David 113
Brown, Tim 137

casinos 112, 115–16
cellphones 4, 25, 49, 51, 65
ceramics 38, 62
Chadwick, Don 43
chairs 5, 27, 43–6, 55, 58, 63
chemistry 39, 51, 134
Coca-Cola 22, 28, 100
co-creation 8, 94, 95, 97, 102, 104–5, 109, 127, 138, 143

co-design 96, 104–5, 119, 122, 125, 130, 132
Colgate 22
collaboration 3, 4, 7, 29, 47, 57, 59, 67, 92, 93, 99, 103, 104, 109, 111, 118, 122, 129, 131, 148
colonialism 109, 110, 146
consumerism 10, 20, 42, 102, 134, 141
Cortana 66
cradle-to-cradle 50, 82
craft 5, 6, 28, 35–6, 47–8, 72, 103, 109, 138, 149
Cross, Nigel 133
crowdfunding 69
crowdsourcing 105
cyberspace 18, 20, 25

Day, Robin 46
decision-making 4, 67, 103, 104, 121–3, 127, 132, 142, 146
decolonization 109, 110, 147
Deloitte 87
Delta 49
dematerialization 51, 55, 114, 144
digitization 35, 52, 95, 103, 106
D'Ignazio, Catherine 31
disability 55, 108–9, 110, 111, 128
disassembly 43, 82
Disney 114–16, 118
disposability 46, 50, 54, 145
Dixon, Tom 48
DIY 47–8
doors 21, 63, 64, 85, 109, 113–14, 145
Dorst, Kees 133
Downe, Louise 95
Dresser, Christopher 38
Droog Design 42
Drucker, Peter 17
Dubois, W.E.B. 29–30
Dunne, Anthony and Fiona Raby 75
Dwiggins, William Addison 19
dystopian 75, 147

Eames, Charles and Ray 125
ecology 27, 51–3, 129
Ehn, Pelle 103
emoji 24–6
empathy 12, 60, 121, 126, 137, 138
Engelbart, Doug 59

Engine Design 86
engineering 6, 7, 10, 13, 29, 49, 51, 54, 57, 58, 65, 67, 75, 122, 123, 126, 149–51
engineers 2, 5–7, 9, 38, 39, 57, 60, 65, 102, 104, 123, 124, 135, 150
EpiPen 61–2
ergonomic 43, 44, 46, 54, 58, 116
ethics 20, 28, 53, 76, 146, 148
ethnography 124, 130, 132, 135, 137, 147
Etsy 35, 47, 72
Expedia 117
Exxon 100

Facebook 23, 104, 106–7, 112, 145
Fairey, Shepard 26
fashion 5, 23, 40, 43, 48, 50, 80, 113, 118
feedback 61, 67, 68, 76, 89, 92
feminism 54, 152, 154, 157
FHWA (Federal Highway Administration) 31–2
font 20, 22–4, 27, 31, 32, 35, 70
Ford, Henry 38–9, 41
Friedman, Bill 115
Frigidaire 100
Frog Design 11, 121
Fry, Tony 146
Fukasawa, Naoto 42
Fuller, Buckminster 82

Galbraith, Jay R. 122
games 33, 66, 67, 70, 74, 76, 91, 104, 106, 115–17, 118
Gap 23
Garland, Ken 20
Garland-Thomson, Rosemarie 108
GDS (Government Design Service) 95
GE 122
gender 54, 66, 76, 89, 102, 145
Gilbert, Phil 126
Gillette 54
GitHub 24
Glaser, Milton 23
globalization 15, 103, 122, 147
Goldsmith, Selwyn 108
Google 24, 26, 28, 68–70, 72, 135
GPS 32, 66, 89, 144

graphs 17, 29, 91
Greenpeace 72
Greyhound 100
GUI 59, 67, 68
Gutenberg 18, 20

hacking 48, 49, 62, 63, 72, 74, 92
Hadid, Zaha 6
hand-crafted 13, 28, 35, 44, 47
Hara, Kenya 27
healthcare 14, 21, 53, 61, 92, 95, 101, 104, 108, 126, 135, 136
Hekkert, Paul 101
Helsinki Design Lab 127–8
Helvetica 2–4, 11, 19, 24, 149
Herman Miller 43, 80
Hom, Lauren 35
human-centered design 8, 53, 60, 64, 67, 86, 122, 136
Human-Computer Interaction (HCI) 57, 65, 102
Human-Robot Interaction (HRI) 57
Hyatt 113

IBM 20, 58, 122, 125–6
icon 4, 23–5, 27, 32, 33, 36, 43, 59, 65, 67, 68, 70, 106, 110
IDEO 11, 121, 135–7
IKEA 48, 49, 74, 80, 83–4
ill-defined 127, 128, 134
inclusive 22, 56, 93, 108, 109, 111, 127, 131, 146
indigenous 23, 24, 94, 108–10, 115, 146, 147
infographics 33–4
Instagram 26, 35, 104, 112, 145
interdisciplinary 7, 11, 57, 65, 76, 99, 117, 119, 137
internet 10, 20, 24, 26, 49, 57, 70–4, 81, 114, 123, 144
Isotype 30, 33
Ive, Jonathan 70

jams 91–2, 132
Jobs, Steve 70
Junginger, Sabine 124

Kalashnikov, Mikhail 3
Kare, Susan 23, 59

Katzumie, Masaru 33
Kees, Dorst 133
Kelley, David 135, 137
Kickstart 52–3
Kickstarter 69
Kimbell, Lucy 86
Kindle 51
Kirkham, Pat 54
Klein, Lauren F. 31
Koefoed, Susanne 110
Kroc, Ray 80
Kurita, Shigetaka 25

laboratories 47, 51, 59, 99, 102, 106, 128, 130–2
Larabie, Raymond 24
Latour, Bruno 62, 64
Laurel, Brenda 66–7
Le Corbusier 39, 58
Lego 50, 80
Levi's 22, 43
LG 73
Linux 104
LiveWork 86
Lockheed 44
Loewy, Raymond 55, 100
logo 2, 5, 8, 13, 17, 19, 20, 22, 23, 26–8, 33, 35, 36, 68, 70, 96, 100, 105, 125
Lufthansa 2
Lyft 88, 89

Mace, Ronald 109
Magistretti, Vico 46
MAKER magazine 47
makerspaces 47–8
Maketools 105
management 8, 10, 17, 62, 81, 85–7, 91, 93, 121–4, 129, 133, 135, 145
manufacturing 6, 9, 10, 12, 13, 38–40, 44, 47, 49, 51, 79, 80, 142, 149
Manzini, Ezio 93–4
Marinovich, Erik 35
Marzano, Stefano 101
Massonet, Henry 46
mass-produced 9, 10, 13, 19, 27, 35, 38–41, 47–50, 53, 54, 55, 56, 58, 72, 86, 99
McDonaldization 80

INDEX

McDonald's 28, 80, 82, 83, 87
McDonough, William 50, 51, 82–3
Microsoft 23, 59, 65, 66, 68, 72, 100
Miedinger, Max 2
MindLab 130–1
MIT 51, 58
Modernization 9, 10, 82, 146
modular 30, 48, 49, 58, 67, 80, 82, 83
Moggridge, Bill 59, 135
Moholy-Nagy, Lazlo 19
Moore, Patricia 55, 109
Morris, William 35
Muji 26–7
multidisciplinary 86, 126, 129, 131, 135, 137

narrative 12, 33, 85, 117, 118, 145, 146
NASA 59
Nelson, George 58
Netflix 79, 81, 100
Neurath, Otto and Marie 30
Newson, Marc 44–5
Nightingale, Florence 29
Nintendo 65, 72
Nokia 49
nonhuman 62, 64, 81, 147, 154
Nooyi, Indra 127
Norman, Donald 60, 61, 63
Noyes, Eliot 58, 125
Nugent, Tim 108
Nuttall, Mike 135
Nygaard, Kristen 103

obsolescence 39, 40, 50, 55, 72, 83
Olivetti 58
Olympics 25, 32, 33, 105
OpenIDEO 136
open-source 24, 104, 127
OXO Good Grips 111
Oxman, Neri 51

packaging 8, 11, 13, 19, 28, 50, 54, 70, 72, 82–4, 114, 127
Pallasmaa, Juhani 63, 64
Panasonic 2
Panton, Vernon 46
Papanek, Victor 53
participatory design 86, 94, 103–6, 109, 119, 122, 125, 131

patent 9, 61, 80, 104
PepsiCo 127
personalization 34, 47, 48, 72, 96, 100, 102
Philips 81–2, 101
pictograms 21, 22, 25, 31, 33
Pinterest 35
Playfair, William 29
policy 8, 15, 83, 96, 106, 121, 124, 129–33, 139, 144, 146
pollution 50, 82, 91, 115, 142
Porcini, Marco 127
posters 2, 6, 9, 17, 19, 26, 35, 36, 117
pre-digital 21, 35, 95
problem-solving 67, 128, 133, 134, 139
Proctor and Gamble 122
propaganda 19, 20
PSS (Product Service System) 81, 82, 96, 128
psychological 14, 43, 58, 91, 101, 150
psychology 57, 60, 65, 99, 101, 135

Rams, Dieter 70
Rand, Paul 20, 125
Rashid, Karim 42
recycling 42, 43, 48, 50, 51, 72, 81, 82, 83, 130
repair 44, 52, 58, 82, 83
repurpose 42, 48, 50, 52, 62, 81
RITA 94
Rittel, Horst 134
Ritzer, George 80
robots 12, 13, 40, 47, 57, 66, 74, 75, 77, 126, 145, 146
Rogal, Maria 109
role-play 55, 87, 104
Rometty, Virginia 126
Roomba 74–5

Samsung 44, 49, 72, 122–4
Sanders, Elizabeth 105
Schifferstein, Hendrik 101
Schrager, Ian 112–13
shanzhai 48–9
Shostack, Lynn G. 85
Siri 66
Sloan, Alfred P. 39
Smart Design 111

Snook Design 131
sociology 29, 80, 99, 101
Sony 81
Sparke, Penny 54
Spiekermann, Erik 36
Spotify 35, 79, 81, 100
standards 7, 32, 44, 49, 54, 76, 108–10, 144
Starbucks 28
Starck, Philippe 42, 112, 113
Steelcase 80
Stevens, Brook 39
storytelling 69, 105, 115, 117, 118
Stottsass, Ettore 58
Stumpf, Bill 43
Subway 28
Sullivan, Louis 4
surveillance 66, 74, 75, 91
sustainability 28, 41, 46, 48, 93, 126, 128, 141
sustainable design 13, 41, 47, 53, 54, 72, 82, 93, 94, 128, 129, 142, 146, 148

taste 2, 13, 20, 45
television 10, 23, 45, 73, 100, 123
Thorvalds, Linus 104
touchpoints 85, 87, 96, 116, 131–2
tourism 32, 85, 94, 109, 112, 116–18
Toyota 2, 40
TripAdvisor 117
Tschichold, Jan 19
Tufte, Edward 30
Tumblr 145
Tupper, Earl 39

Twitter 104
typography 18, 19, 27, 28, 30, 31, 33, 35, 54, 67, 84, 85, 95

Uber 88–91
unsustainability 15, 50, 143
urbanization 9, 12
user-centered design 60, 94, 101, 106, 121, 131, 135, 137, 138, 156
utopia 39, 103, 144
utopian 75, 147

Van Doren, Harold 39
Verplank, Bill 59
Virgin Airlines 86–7
VISA 22
visualization 12, 13, 24, 29–34, 36, 94, 122, 131, 137, 148
voice-controlled 32, 66, 75

Walker, Stuart 146
Warde, Beatrice 18
Watson, Thomas Jr. 58, 125
wayfinding 31, 32, 36, 80, 87, 108, 110
WeChat 145
WhatsApp 145
Wright, Frank Lloyd 6

Xerox Parc 58, 59

Yamashita, Yoshiro 33
Youtube 70, 74

Zara 80
Zuckerberg, Mark 107

Milton Keynes UK
Ingram Content Group UK Ltd.
UKHW020841121224
452339UK00004B/241